Hopi History in Stone

The Tutuveni Petroglyph Site

Wesley Bernardini

Arizona State Museum
THE UNIVERSITY OF ARIZONA.

Arizona State Museum Archaeological Series 200

Arizona State Museum
The University of Arizona
Tucson, Arizona 85721-0026
© 2007, 2015 by the Arizona Board of Regents
All rights reserved. First edition 2007. Second edition 2015.
Printed in the United States of America

ISBN (paper): 978-1-889747-82-8
ISBN (reprint): 978-1-889747-97-2

Library of Congress Control Number: 2007942111
Library of Congress Control Number (reprint): 2015954856

ARIZONA STATE MUSEUM ARCHAEOLOGICAL SERIES

General Editor: Richard C. Lange
Technical Editors: Lauren E. Jelinek, Alicia M. Vega

The *Archaeological Series* of the Arizona State Museum, The University of Arizona, publishes the results of research in archaeology and related disciplines conducted in the Greater Southwest. Original, monograph-length manuscripts are considered for publication, provided they deal with appropriate subject matter. Information regarding procedures or manuscript submission and review may be obtained from the General Editor, *Archaeological Series*, Arizona State Museum, P.O. Box 210026, The University of Arizona, Tucson, Arizona, 85721-0026; Email: langer@email.arizona.edu.

On the cover is an illustration of petroglyph elements on the southeast panel of Boulder 48, see Figures II.68 and II.69 in the text.

Distributed by The University of Arizona Press, 355 S. Euclid Boulevard, Suite 103, Tucson, Arizona 85719

Contents

List of Tables

Contents of Companion DVD

Figures (folder of images)
      Appendix Figures (figures in Appendix I)
      Text Figures (figures appearing in the text)
Images (folder of images)
      2004 Documentation Photos (photographs from the 2004 formal documentation)
      Historic Photos (photographs taken at other times before and after 2004)
XXXXX (folder of images showing how the documentation was done and indexing the elements recorded)
Look At Me (a folder with *.doc, *.pdf, and *.txt versions of a document describing how the DVD is organized)
File Descriptions 2004 Documentation Photos (*.pdf and Excel versions indexing the 2004 photos)
File Descriptions Historic Photos (*.pdf and Excel versions indexing the other photos)
Tutuveni Element Database (*.pdf and Excel versions indexing the elements present at the site)

Preface and Acknowledgments

PREFACE

The Tutuveni Petroglyph site is a potential Rosetta Stone of Hopi clan iconography, containing the largest, most significant concentration of clan symbols found anywhere in the American Southwest, in any medium. It constitutes an invaluable resource for interpreting petroglyphs across the Pueblo world. With more than 200 line drawings and more than 2,500 photographs spanning 75 years, this book presents a comprehensive record of the Tutuveni petroglyphs, ensuring that their historical information will be preserved for future generations of scholars, Native Americans, and the public. The Tutuveni project was the result of a collaborative effort between academic archaeologists and the Hopi and Navajo Tribes, united in a common interest to document this important cultural resource before it was damaged irreparably by vandalism. This preservation research is a model for a new type of archaeology, illustrating the mutual benefits of collaboration between archaeologists and descendant communities.

Technical Issues

A DVD was included with the original publication of this volume (2007). On the DVD were folders that contained all of the photographs from the text. In addition, the DVD contained a large number of figures that are cited in the text, but do not appear in print, which are labeled DVD####. These DVD-only figures are listed in the Table of Contents and comprise both historical and recent photographs of the Tutuveni site. The DVD also included a Microsoft Excel spreadsheet containing a database of all tabulated petroglyph symbols at Tutuveni.

There is no DVD in this version of the volume (Fall, 2015), but all of these images and materials are accessible on the Arizona State Museum website under:

www.statemuseum.arizona.edu/pubs/archseries/companion_materials.html

Project records and photographs from the 2004 Tutuveni recording project are curated at the University of Redlands and the Hopi Cultural Preservation Office in Kykotsmovi, Arizona. A complete set of historical and recent photographs is also archived in digital form at the Navajo Historic Preservation Office in Window Rock, Arizona.

ACKNOWLEDGMENTS

I am grateful for the support provided by the Hopi Cultural Preservation Office staff during this project, including Leigh Kuwanwisiwma, Lanell Poseyesva, Lee Wayne Lomayestewa, Sue Kuyvaya, Micah Lomaomvaya, Stewart Koyiyumptewa, and Sharon Sockyma. In addition, this project would not have been possible without the assistance of the Navajo Historic Preservation Department, where Ronald Maldonado was especially helpful. The University of Redlands provided financial and logistical support for my fieldwork. I gratefully acknowledge the generosity of several researchers who shared data and advice, including Sylvia Gaines, Evelyn Billo, Robert Marks, Patricia McCreery, and Donald Weaver. The assistance of the Museum of Northern Arizona (MNA) and the UCLA Rock Art Archive was also critical to the success of this project. I am grateful for helpful comments on the manuscript provided by T. J. Ferguson, Andrew Duff, and E. Charles Adams. Finally, many thanks go to the University of Redlands students who worked hard to complete this project in the field and in the lab, including Larry Aguirre, Katie Hammond, Elizabeth Madrid, Michelle Newman, Molly Stroud, Laura Tencati, and especially Anna Ashbrook, Elizabeth Hora, and Josh Kleinman.

Chapter One
Tutuveni in Context

Rock art is notoriously difficult to interpret (Morphy 1989). Part of the difficulty stems from the use of the term art, which is loaded with western notions of the opaque creative impulse of individual artists. Yet cultural advisors agree that petrolyphs can be symbolically complex, suggesting that "a diversity of practices, purposes, and meanings applies to this particular medium of expression" (Young 1988:91). In this light, the Tutuveni Petroglyph site is distinctive for its *lack* of ambiguity, for the site consists almost exclusively of a single, well-interpreted type of image: clan symbols.

Clans are a hallmark of contemporary Hopi life, and are the medium through which much Hopi traditional knowledge is transmitted. Many scholars agree that clan-like groups may have been part of Pueblo social organization in the past (Bernardini 2005a, 2005b; Eggan 1950; Ferguson and Lomaomvaya 1999; Lyons 2003; Steward 1937). Long recognized similarities between contemporary Hopi clan symbols and some ancient petroglyphs (Fewkes 1892; Turner 1963) indicate that there is the potential to trace clans back in time, in the process bringing together information about the past from both traditional knowledge and archaeology e.g., Bernardini 2005a). Southwestern researchers have tried to use clan iconography to track the migrations of ancient Hopi clans across the landscape since the time of Jesse Walter Fewkes (Fewkes 1900), but have been hindered by several problems. A primary obstacle has been the lack of a systematic and ethnographically grounded inventory of clan symbol iconography. In the absence of such an inventory -- or without tribal consultation on each petrolyph site -- it can be difficult to separate ancient images that were intended to symbolize clan marks from those intended to convey a myriad of other symbolic messages. Complicating the identification of ancient clan symbols is the fact that not all of the clans that existed in the American Southwest over the past 1,000 years have living descendants who can identify their clan marks. The demographic crashes of the late 1800s, as well as the epidemics that wiped out large portions of Pueblo populations in the period following Spanish contact, surely caused the extinction of many clans. Even in the absence of such crises, regular variation in mortality and fertility rates would result in the loss of many small lineage groups (Gaines and Gaines 1997).

In this light, the extraordinary value of the Tutuveni Petroglyph site stems from the fact that it can be used as a Rosetta Stone of sorts, "translating" the Hopi clan symbols present in rock art across the American Southwest. Tutuveni can serve this function because it contains a continuous record of clan symbols stretching from the early twentieth century back 500 years or more. During this span of time, the style of the images at Tutuveni remained remarkably consistent: iconic symbols, typically of recognizable animals, plants, or cultural items, of moderate size (about 10x10 cm), arranged into rows of repeated symbols. This style characterizes both the oldest, most repatinated panels, and the youngest, least repatinated ones. Almost completely lacking are the narrative panels, elaborate anthropomorphic figures, and complicated geometric patterns that have proved so resistant to straightforward interpretation at other petroglyph sites in the region. Many of the petroglyphs at Tutuveni correspond to the marks of living Hopi clans, and the majority of those that do not are so similar in style and arrangement to contemporary clan symbols that both cultural insiders and outsiders interpret them as markers of extinct clans (Colton and Colton 1931). While the assemblage of clan symbols at Tutuveni does not necessarily include all Hopi clans of the past 500 years, it contains the largest, most significant concentration of Puebloan clan symbols to be found anywhere in the Southwest, in any medium.

GEOGRAPHIC AND POLITICAL CONTEXT

The Tutuveni Petroglyph site, variously recorded as Willow Springs, Oakley Springs, NA 4492, and NA 994, is located in Coconino County, Arizona, near the town of Munqapi, also known as Moenkopi (Fig. 1.1). The site, which covers a boulder-strewn slope at the base of the Echo Cliffs (Fig. 1.2), is situated near

a number of perennial springs, making it "a focal point through which nearly all sojourners through the area would pass" (Tessman 1986:4). Petroglyphs completely cover the sides and tops of a number of large sandstone blocks at the base of the slope, and are found sporadically on the surfaces of more than 100 additional boulders along a 150 meter-long north-south swath.

The Tutuveni Petroglyph site is located in an unusual and highly charged socio-geographic position. The area around Tutuveni has been the subject of a longstanding dispute over land claims and reservation boundaries between the Hopi Tribe and Navajo Nation, dating back more than a century (Brugge 1994). The Hopi Tribe identifies Tutuveni as a Hopi shrine, a claim recognized by the National Register of Historic Places (Tessman 1986:7) and by the Navajo Historic Preservation Office, under agreements regarding Hopi/Navajo Partitioned Lands. However, the site is technically on Navajo land and is 35 km from the western boundary of the primary Hopi reservation. A small island of Hopi land is also associated with the Hopi village of Munqapi, about 13 km from Tutuveni (Fig. 1.1). Tutuveni's location, combined with the unusually clear expressions of Hopi cultural identity which are materialized at the site, have made it a target of those who

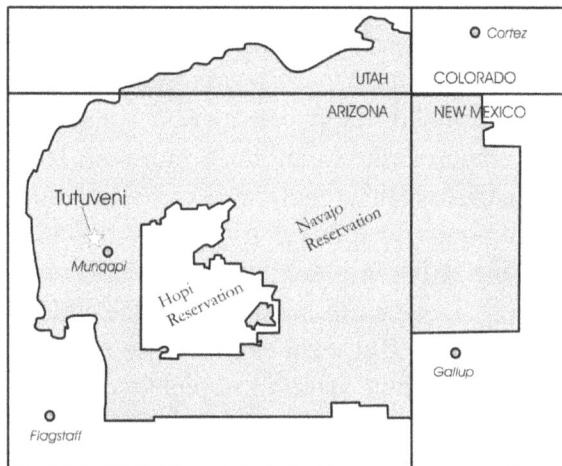

Figure 1.1. Location of the Tutuveni Petroglyph site.

Figure 1.2. Overview of Tutuveni, looking east; DVD2556.

take issue with Hopi historical claims on the surrounding area. The site has suffered from vandalism, especially the targeted destruction of symbols perhaps deemed by visitors to tell the wrong version of history (see Chapter 4). By 2008 the vandalism to Tutuveni had become so severe that the site was placed on the World Monuments Watch List of 100 Most Endangered Sites (http://wmf.org/watch/html).

In spite of the politically charged landscape surrounding Tutuveni and the history of vandalism at the site, the story behind this book is one of collaboration and cooperation between the Hopi Tribe and the Navajo Nation, and between academic archaeology and descendant communities. All parties agreed that recent vandalism at Tutuveni threatened an important cultural resource, and it was a mutual concern for the protection of this resource that led to the preservation research detailed in this book. Archaeological fieldwork was preceded by intensive discussions with representatives from the Hopi Cultural Preservation Office, who stressed the importance of Tutuveni as a vehicle for cultural instruction for younger generations about Hopi clan history. Interpretation of Tutuveni by the Hopi was guided by members of the Hopi Cultural Resources Advisory Task Team (CRATT), representing the third major episode of collaborative interpretation of the site by the Hopi and archaeologists over the past 75 years (see Chapter 3). Parallel, but less intense, consultation with the Navajo Nation was also conducted, though further research is warranted to more fully document Navajo perspectives on the area around Tutuveni. This type of research, in which descendant communities do not simply approve existing research designs, but actively shape research questions and methods, may be critical to the future viability of Southwestern archaeology (Colwell-Chanthaphonh and Ferguson 2006; Swidler and others 1997).

ETHNOGRAPHIC CONTEXT

The petroglyphs at Tutuveni are well interpreted with regard to function because Hopi clans were still using the site during the early part of the twentieth century, when anthropologists could record the production of new petroglyphs alongside morphologically similar older ones. Ethnographic observations document that Tutuveni was, and continues to be, an important Hopi shrine, serving as a designated stopping point on a trail leading from Third Mesa to *Öngtupqa*, the Grand Canyon (Ferguson 1998:186–192; Titiev 1937; Weaver 1984). Historically, participants in the Hopi tribal initiation ceremony, the *Wuwtsim* (see Fig. 1.3), followed this trail to collect salt from the canyon. At Tutuveni, each initiate marked his participation in the salt gathering trip by pecking his clan symbol into a boulder, typically in a row next to his clansmen's previous symbols. Thus, the site consists of many hundreds of rows of clan symbols, covering portions of 154 separate boulders.

Wuwtsim

Prior to the 1940s, virtually all Hopi men underwent *Wuwtsim* initiation between adolescence and marriage (Titiev 1944:130). The *Wuwtsim* was "like a birth into adult life" (Frigout 1979:573; see also Whiteley 1988:195) and may be considered a literal tribal initiation for men (Parsons 1923:181).

Titiev (1944:130) called the *Wuwtsim* "the most complicated, and among the most vital of all Hopi ceremonies." Knowledge of this ceremony outside the tribe has been intentionally limited by preventing ethnographers, even the aggressive Alexander Stephen, from viewing key parts of the proceedings (Eggan 1950:51; Parsons 1936:977). In general ethnographers believe that the *Wuwtsim* teaches initiates

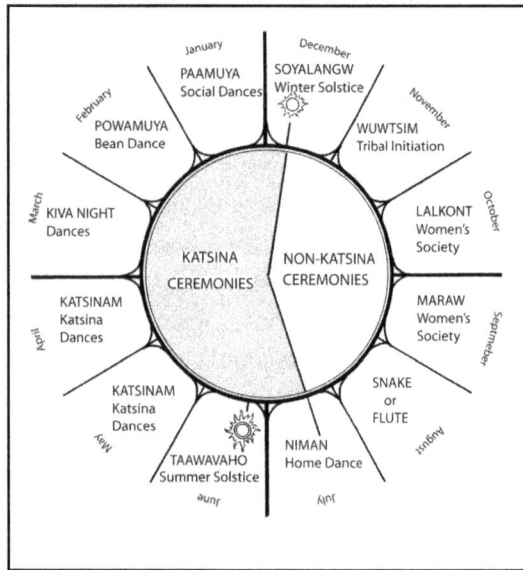

Figure 1.3. The Hopi ceremonial calendar, adapted from Wright (1977:7) and Ferguson and Lomaomvaya (1999:Figure 10).

about the emergence of the Hopi from the *Sipaapuni*, which is "both the orifice through which man came forth on earth," and also "the direct entrance to the Underworld [*Maski*]" (Titiev 1944:134). The *Sipaapuni* is located in the Grand Canyon, *Öngtupqa*, which gives the *Wuwtsim* its assocation with the canyon.

Completion of the *Wuwtsim* initiation required a lengthy and dangerous pilgrimage down into *Öngtupqa* to gather salt. The journey to *Öngtupqa* was hazardous not just for the close proximity to *Maski* (Bradfield 1973:45), but also the precarious descent into the Grand Canyon, by means of ropes and pecked hand-and-foot-holds. Furthermore, during the historical period the possibility of encountering hostile Navajos brought significant danger (Titiev 1937:245). The hazards of the journey comprised a "test of manhood and opportunity to purify the new *Wuwtsim* initiate" (Ferguson 1998:55).

The Hopi pilgrimages to *Öngtupqa*, associated with the *Wuwtsim*, have often been called "salt pilgrimages" (Titiev 1937), but as Eiseman (1959:31) noted:

…the Hopi do not regard the obtaining of salt as the really important feature of a salt-gathering expedition. The expedition is made into a very sacred place, full of dangers and fears. To come through the attendant rituals, to visit the original *sipapu*, to make offerings at the many shrines, all these would bring the participant good luck and happiness. The salt itself appears to be a tangible piece of evidence that one had made the trip successfully and with a good heart. The village always welcomed the successful salt gatherers, feeling that the whole village would benefit from the offerings made to the gods, and from the good things accruing to those who made the trip.

Men from Third Mesa, and occasionally Second Mesa, traditionally undertook the salt pilgrimage to *Öngtupqa* (Harvey 1970:70–71; Simmons 1942:232–246; Titiev 1937). First Mesa men, and presumably Antelope Mesa men prior to the end of their year-round residence on that mesa in A.D. 1700, typically traveled to Zuni Salt Lake as part of their *Wuwtsim* initiations, although Hopi cultural advisors note that men from Second Mesa and First Mesa have also gathered salt from *Öngtupqa* during the historic period (Ferguson 1998). Thus, the clan symbols at Tutuveni are likely dominated by Third Mesa clans, but also include some Second, First, and possibly Antelope Mesa clan symbols.

The last recorded salt gathering trip to *Öngtupqa* took place sometime in the late 1950s or early 1960s (Balsom 1993:12; Waters 1963:146), although both the *Wuwtsim* initiation and the *Öngtupqa* pilgrimage had ceased being performed regularly on Third Mesa after the breakup of the village of Orayvi in 1906. The last documented pilgrimage to *Öngtupqa* associated with a *Wuwtsim* initiation took place in 1911 or 1912 (Simmons 1942:232–246; Titiev 1937:244).

Previous Research

Tutuveni has been visited and recorded in varying detail by Euro-Americans for over 100 years (Colton 1946, 1960; Eiseman 1959; Mallery 1886; McNitt 1964; Michaelis 1981; and Titiev 1937). An 1878 visit to Tutuveni by G. K. Gilbert resulted in the first published description of the site (Mallery 1886). Mallery also published a sketch of the southeast face of boulder 48 (Mallery 1886: Figure 1). Gilbert reported being told by Tuuvi, the Orayvi Chief, after whom the nearby town of Tuba City is named, that:

> Mokis [Hopis] make excursions to a locality in the canyon of the Colorado Chiquito [the Grand Canyon] to get salt. On their return they stop at Oakley Spring [Tutuveni] and each Indian makes a picture on the rock. Each Indian draws his crest or totem, the symbol of his gens. He draws it once, and once only, each visit [Mallery 1886:29].

In 1930 Harold and Mary Colton visited the site along with Hopi consultant Edmund Nequatewa. Colton's photographs from this visit are curated at the Museum of Northern Arizona (MNA) and represent the earliest known photographic record of Tutuveni. During his visit, Harold Colton sketched a number of symbols, which were identified for him by Edmund Nequatewa. The Coltons' visits to Tutuveni were written up in a series of short articles and book chapters (Colton and Colton 1931; Colton 1946; Colton 1960).

In the mid-1930s Misha Titiev (1937) recorded an account of a 1912 salt pilgrimage from Don Talayesva, a Hopi Sun Clan member. Talayesva's 1942 autobiography *Sun Chief*

(Simmons 1942) contains another account of this trip. Talayesva provided a detailed description of the journey and the actions taken at each stopping place, including a stop at Tutuveni where "each man was supposed to carve his clan emblem on the rocky face of the shrine, and on each successive visit to repeat the device to the left of his original 'signature'" (Titiev 1937:245–6). Talayesva noted that the salt trail includes more than 30 named stopping places, each associated with a different aspect of Hopi cosmology.

In 1958 Fred Eiseman followed the Hopi salt trail from Tutuveni into the Grand Canyon using landmarks provided in Talayesva's autobiography (Simmons 1942), locating a number of shrines, petroglyphs, and ladders leading to a travertine dome in the bottom of the canyon. Samples of the surrounding salt deposits were taken and shown to Hopi consultants, who confirmed their provenience.

In a series of popular articles in the 1960s and 1970s, Mildred and C. R. Hooper (1968; 1977) described Tutuveni, which they called Willow Springs. The Hoopers investigated Mormon inscriptions at the site and learned of a Mormon missionary named H. K. Perkins, who led a group from Salt Lake City through Lee's Ferry to Willow Springs in 1873. An inscription by Perkins can be found on the top face of boulder 56. Subsequent Mormon parties left inscriptions in adjacent canyons and near the remains of later trading posts approximately half a mile north of Tutuveni. The Hoopers also identified 17 clan symbols with the assistance of two Hopi women from Polacca village, Nellie Douma of the Corn Clan and Hilda Nahee from the Tobacco Clan.

Between 1976 and 1980 amateur archaeologist Helen Michaelis undertook the only previous attempt to systematically record the petroglyphs at Tutuveni. Her work began in response to vandalism to the site in the 1970s, the accelerated pace of which also motivated the current study (see Chapter 4). Michaelis photographed 41 boulders, from which 2,178 individual clan symbols were tallied. Using these symbols, lists of Hopi clans, and Nequatewa's clan symbol identifications published by Colton (Colton and Colton 1931; Colton 1946; Colton 1960), Michaelis identified the symbols of 32 clans. Unfortunately, upon Michealis' death many of her field notes and photographs were lost, and only a small selection of photographs and a brief report are curated at the UCLA Rock Art Archive.

In 1986 Tutuveni was listed on the National Register of Historic Places. The nomination form notes that "[Tutuveni] is apparently unique [among Southwestern petroglyph sites] in being well interpreted in function, and pertaining to a specific, well documented event, the Hopi Salt Pilgrimage to the Grand Canyon" (Tessman 1986:5). In 1998 the Hopi Cultural Preservation Office published an ethnohistoric report on Hopi ties to the Grand Canyon, which included information on Tutuveni (Ferguson 1998). Interviews with Hopi cultural advisors conducted for that report documented extensive Hopi traditional knowledge of the area.

Bernardini (2005a, 2005b) used the petroglyphs at Tutuveni as a database of Hopi clan symbols against which petroglyphs from other areas of the Southwest could be compared. The presence of petroglyphs resembling clan symbols at Tutuveni at fourteenth century sites in central Arizona was interpreted as support for Hopi migration traditions, which recount the presence of ancestral Hopi populations in these villages (see Chapter 5).

CHRONOLOGICAL CONTEXT

As is the case with most petroglyph sites, it is difficult to estimate the age of the symbols at Tutuveni. The Tutuveni petroglyphs cannot yet be directly dated, but a variety of lines of evidence suggest use of the site for at least 500 years, most likely beginning in the Pueblo IV period (ca. A.D. 1300–1540).

The area immediately surrounding the site has a dearth of datable artifacts. An intensive survey of a 100 m radius area around the site revealed only 12 sherds (Fig. 1.4) and no lithic material, although heavy visitation over the past two decades may account for the paucity of painted ceramics. The area is also surrounded by active sand deposits, which would rapidly bury most surface artifacts. The 12 recorded sherds consist of eight badly eroded Tsegi Orange Ware sherds (A.D. 1000–1300), three Black Mesa Black-on-White sherds (A.D. 1025–1150), and one Sosi Black-on-White sherd (A.D. 1075–1200). None of the ceramics were found in direct association with petroglyph-bearing boulders; however, the assemblage does indicate that the area was in use by Ancestral Puebloan populations from at least the mid A.D. 1000s. A search of the archaeological site files at the MNA revealed that the closest recorded residential site to Tutuveni is the Moenave Ruin (NA 48), a masonry pueblo consisting of approximately 50 rooms atop an isolated mesa, located approximately one mile to the south. A non-systematic review of surface ceramics at NA 48 suggests that it was occupied during approximately A.D. 1150–1250.

The degree of repatination on the Tutuveni petroglyphs provides a relative indication of their age. Petroglyphs are created through the removal of the manganese-rich patina, known as desert varnish, which accumulates over time on the surface of some types of rock. Once the lighter colored underlying rock beneath the patina is exposed it begins to repatinate, so that the color difference between the petroglyph and the surrounding rock is an indicator of the relative age of the petroglyph. Repatination at Tutuveni ranges from almost completely repatinated symbols to very fresh ones. Petroglyphs at Tutuveni photographed by Harold Colton in 1930 show very little change in patination over the ensuing 75 years, suggesting that the heavy repatination of the petroglyphs on some boulders, such as boulder 48, likely required many hundreds of years of exposure.

Repatination was recorded at Tutuveni on an ordinal scale using four categories: absent, light, moderate, and heavy. A complicating factor is the fact that many petroglyphs have been repecked or "renovated" at least once over the past century (Cheremisin 2002; Hedges 1990), an observation made by comparing contemporary and historical photographs (see Chapter 3). The repatination designations in this analysis all refer to the condition of the boulder in the earliest available historical image, usually either 1930 or 1978. However, because historical photographs are not available for all panels, it was not always possible to determine conclusively whether repecking

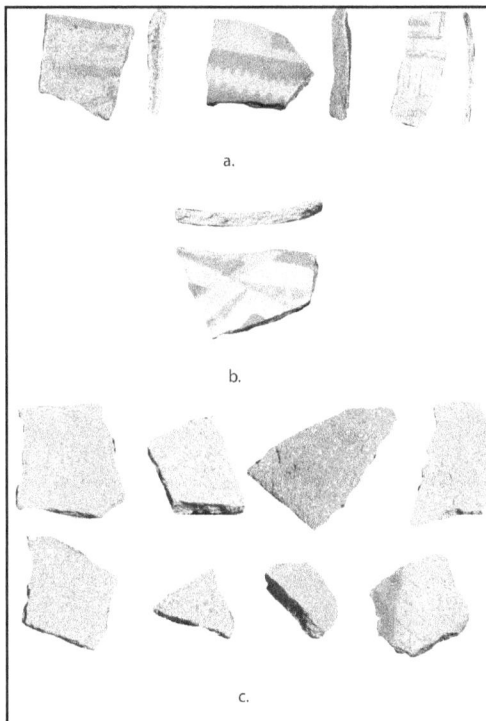

Figure 1.4. Ceramics associated with Tutuveni. a. Black Mesa Black-on-white, b. Sosi Black-on-white, c. Tsegi Orange Ware (badly eroded).

had occurred.

As is evident in Figure 1.5, the most heavily repatinated boulders are concentrated at the western edge of the site. The most heavily repatinated symbols are found on the largest, central rock, boulder 48, which also contains the largest number of symbols of now extinct clans (see Chapter 3). Seven additional boulders surrounding boulder 48, including boulders 8, 14, 17, 18, 30, 34, and 55, contain the majority of the remaining heavily and moderately repatinated symbols, as well as the largest number of symbols. This group of eight boulders comprises the core of the site.

The style of the vast majority of the Tutuveni petroglyphs conforms to Glen Canyon Style 2 (Turner 1963); in fact, Tutuveni is identified as a type site for this style. Style 2 is found most commonly on the Hopi Mesas, and is linked to production by historical or ancestral Hopi groups. Turner (1963) notes that Style 2 petroglyphs are closely associated with post-A.D. 1300 Hopi ceramics (Jeddito Yellow Ware), suggesting a Pueblo IV period date-range (ca. A.D. 1300–1540) for these designs. Tutuveni contains no earlier petroglyph styles (Style 3–5), but does include a number of Style 1 (historical Navajo, Paiute, and Anglo) elements. These Style 1 elements are readily distinguished on the basis of technique (engraved, scratched, or lightly and sloppily pecked) and content (sheep, horses, cowboys, and English words, names, and dates) (Turner 1963:5).

ORGANIZATION OF THE VOLUME

Having placed Tutuveni in a geographic, ethnographic, and chronological context, the remainder of this volume presents and analyzes the data from the site. Chapter 2 discusses Hopi clans and clan symbols, and the historical problems in nomenclature that stem from the confusion of clans with their clan totems.

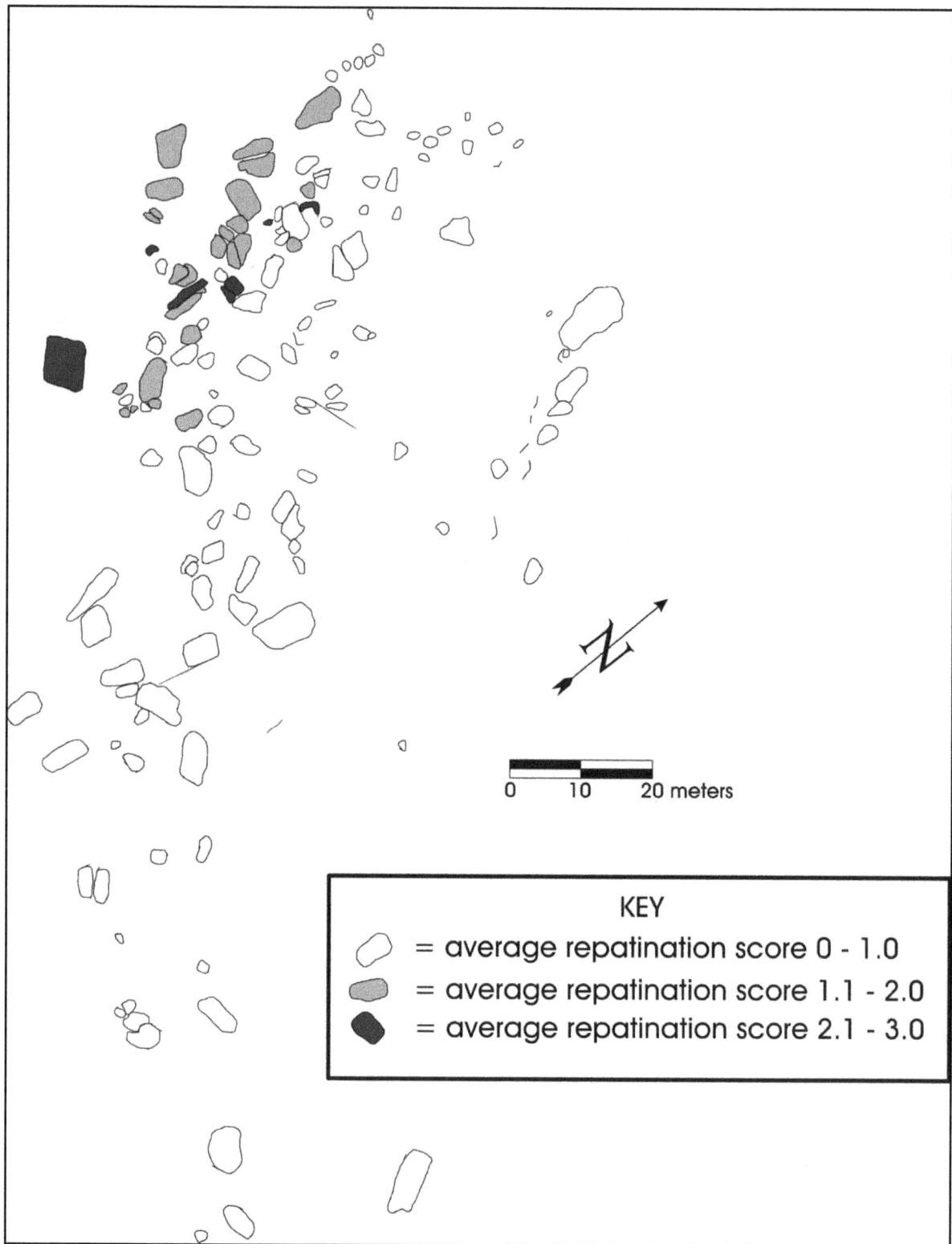

Figure 1.5. Average repatination scores for panels at Tutuveni: no repatination, 0–1.0 = light repatination, 1.1–2.0 = moderate repatination, 2.1–3.0 = heavy repatination.

Chapter 3 explains the procedures employed in the mapping, field recording, and lab analysis of the Tutuveni petroglyphs, including information from almost 800 historical photographs, and presents line drawings and photographs of the primary panels containing clan symbols. Patterns of symbol frequency and distribution across the site are then presented, including a quantification of the number of visits per clan and the identification of symbols of extinct clans. Chapter 4 discusses vandalism at the Tutuveni site, establishing a timeline of damage, reconstructing damaged boulders from historical photographs, and discussing the political context in which the damage occurred. Chapter 5 concludes the volume with thoughts on the importance of Tutuveni in southwestern archaeology, including comparisons to regions away from the Hopi Mesas exhibiting potential Hopi clan symbols. Finally, the DVD attached to the back cover of the book includes a spreadsheet tabulating each of the 5,103 symbols recorded at the site, line drawings of all 235 petroglyph panels, and more than 2,500 digital photographs of Tutuveni spanning the period from 1930 to 2005.

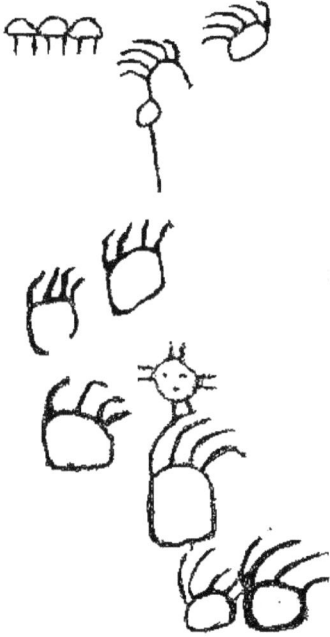

Chapter Two
Clans and Clan Symbols

The word clan is a heavily loaded term in Southwestern anthropology and in the discipline as a whole, having been used in a number of contexts to refer to different kinds of social groups (Lowie 1929; Murdock 1949; Parsons 1925). The classic ethnographic descriptions of Hopi clans were made by Titiev (1944) and Eggan (1950); important recent treatments of Hopi clans may be found in Connelly (1979), Levy (1992), and especially Whiteley (1985, 1986, 1988). This chapter will not attempt a comprehensive review of the literature on Hopi clans, but the centrality of clans to the current study mandates some clarification about their composition, discreteness, and symbolism. The primary purpose of this discussion is to clarify the relationship between the clan as a social group and the clan symbols used to represent that group.

WHAT IS A CLAN?

The ethnographic definition of a Hopi clan is a group of people united through the female line sharing a totemic affiliation with an object or aspect of nature, for example, the Bow clan or Bear clan. According to Hopi traditional knowledge, totemic affiliations were acquired during the clans' migrations in search of *Tuuwanasavi*, the earth center on the Hopi Mesas (Dongoske and others 1997:603). In the early 20th century, most Hopi clans controlled a ceremony, and the importance of this ceremony in the ritual cycle of the village was an important component of clan status (Levy 1992).

Disagreements among anthropologists about the nature of Hopi clans have focused on two issues: 1) the degree to which clans operate as corporate (that is, unified) groups, and 2) the relationship of clans to smaller and larger social units. According to the conventional ethnographic view established by Titiev (1944) and Eggan (1950), Hopi society is organized into a series of increasingly inclusive matrilineal descent groups, including households, lineages, clans, and phratries. The clan is the only named unit of this series, and is "the outstanding feature of social life, in Hopi eyes" (Eggan 1950:62). A clan is organized around the household of the senior woman, and may contain up to several lineages of daughters' families. In this conventional view, clans are arranged into larger, unnamed, but exogamous, groupings called phratries. The Hopi Cultural Preservation Office has compiled a list of 62 current and recently extinct Hopi clans found on the three occupied Hopi Mesas, arranged into 11 phratries (Table 2.1). However, almost every Hopi ethnographer has compiled a different list of clans arranged into slightly different groupings (e.g., Lowie 1929:330, 332; Mindeleff 1891:651; Titiev 1944:Chart VI; White 1944 [cited in Titiev 1944:Table 1]).

Early Hopi ethnographers emphasized the corporate control of resources by clans, but subsequent research has shown that certain resources, particularly ritual knowledge,

Table 2.1. Hopi Clans Organized by English Gloss (data from Leigh J. Kuwanwisiwma, Peter Whiteley, Micah Lomaomvaya, and T. J. Ferguson; on file at the Hopi Cultural Preservation Office).

English Gloss	Mesa	Hopi Name	Phratry
Agave Clan		*Kwanngyam*	10
Antelope Clan	First and Second	*Tsövngyam*	
Antelope Clan	Third	*Tsöpngyam*	
Arrow Clan	First	*Hoongyam*	4
Arrow Clan	Third	*Hoongyam*	5
Badger Clan		*Honanngyam*	7
Bean Seed Clan		*Morivosngyam*	
Bear Clan		*Honngyam*	2
Bearstrap Clan		*Piqösngyam*	2
Black Throated Sparrow Clan		*Kookopngyam*	6
Blue Flute Clan		*Sakwalenngyam*	
Bluebird Clan		*Tsorngyam*	2
Bow Clan		*Aawatngyam*	5
Burrowing Owl Clan		*Kokootngyam*	
Butterfly Clan		*Poovolngyam (Polingyam)*	7
Chakwaina Clan		*Tsa'kwaynangyam*	11
Cloud Clan		*Oomawngyam*	
Collared Lizard Clan		*Manangyam*	
Corn Clan		*Qa'öngyam*	8
Cottontail Rabbit Clan	First and Third	*Tapngyam*	1
Cottontail Rabbit Clan	Second	*Tavngyam*	1
Coyote Clan		*Isngyam*	6
Crane Clan		*Atokngyam*	9
Duck/Aquatic Bird		*Paawikwngyam*	8
Eagle Clan		*Kwaangyam*	4
Flute Clan		*Lenngyam*	10
Fog Clan		*Paamösngyam*	
Frog Clan		*Paakwangyam*	8
Gray Badger Clan		*Masihonanngyam*	7
Gray Flute Clan		*Masilenngyam*	
Gray Hawk Clan		*Masikwayngyam*	4
Greasewood	First and Second	*Tevngyam*	5
Greasewood	Third	*Tepngyam*	5
Horn/Deer Clan		*Alngyam*	10

are distributed very unequally within a clan (Whiteley 1985, 1986). Ceremonial offices and knowledge are held "not in the clan as a whole, but in a maternal family or lineage in the clan" (Parsons 1933:23). It is "through the performance of one's clan-ascribed ceremonial duties as much as through anything else that one feels oneself a part of Hopi society" (Schlegel 1992:382), making proximity to the seat of ritual knowledge important for one's clan identity. As a consequence, depending upon who is asked, clan assignments can become "loaded

Table 2.1. Hopi Clans Organized by English Gloss (data from Leigh J. Kuwanwisiwma, Peter Whiteley, Micah Lomaomvaya, and T. J. Ferguson; on file at the Hopi Cultural Preservation Office), cont'd.

English Gloss	Mesa	Hopi Name	Phratry
Immature Corn Clan		*Piikyasngyam*	8
Indian Rice Grass Clan		*Leengyam*	6
Jackrabbit Clan		*Sowi'ngyam*	1
Katsina Clan		*Katsinngyam*	1
Lightning Clan		*Talwiipikw'ngyam*	8
Lizard Clan		*Kuukutsngyam*	3
Lizard Clan		*Naanawngyam*	
Máasaw Clan		*Masngyam*	6
Mountain Sheep Clan		*Pangwu'ngyam*	
Mud Clan		*Tsöqangyam*	
Parrot Clan		*Kyarngyam*	1
Pipe Clan		*Tsoongongyam*	
Rabbitbrush Clan		*Sivap'ngyam*	
Rainbow Clan		*Tangaqapngyam*	8
Rattlesnake Clan		*Tsu'ngyam*	3
Raven/Crow Clan		*Angwusngyam*	1
Reed Clan	First	*Paaqapngyam*	4
Reed Clan	Third	*Paaqapngyam*	5
Roadrunner Clan		*Hospo'ngyam*	
Sand Clan		*Tuwangyam*	3
Sparrow Hawk/Kestrel Clan		*Kyelngyam*	9
Spider Clan		*Kookyangngyam*	2
Squash Clan		*Paatangngyam*	9
Sun Clan		*Taawangyam*	4
Sun Forehead		*Qalngyam*	4
Tadpole Clan		*Paavatngyam*	8
Tansy Mustard Clan		*Asngyam*	5
Tobacco Clan	First and Second	*Pifngyam*	1
Tobacco Clan	Third	*Pipngyam*	1
Water Clan		*Patkingyam*	8
Water Coyote (Desert Fox)		*Paa'isngyam*	6
Watermelon Clan		*Kawayvatngyam*	
White Sand Clan		*Pisangyam*	
Young Corn Clan		*Piikyasngyam*	8

with political and social considerations which have nothing to do with genealogy" (Whiteley 2003:165).

Problems with the classification of Hopi clans were noted early on by ethnographers, whose interviews with Hopi consultants pro-duced lists of clans with different names for the same group, and lists of individuals who were assigned to differently named groups by different consultants (Titiev 1944:48). Eggan (1950:63) noted that "sixty to one hundred or more [clan] names may be furnished by informants living in villages in which only a handful of clans actually exist" (Eggan 1950:63).

Titiev (1944:53) noted that contradictory clan assignments tended to fall consistently within a small grouping of related clans, a unit he termed a phratry. Hopi consultants agreed that the groups within Eggan's phratries were partners, having shared migration experiences, and noted that phratry members could use the totem of any partner clans to symbolize their clan identity. The cultural advisors, however, sometimes grouped partner clans under a single totemic name, creating terminological confusion, as explained by Whiteley (2003:165, emphasis and parentheses in original):

> It was…unclear whether '-*ngyam*,' [the plural Hopi suffix for a matrilineal descent group]… was more appropriately considered as naming the maximal exogamous set or its more specific components. For example if, in Hopi speech, *Honngyam*, 'Bear' *ngyam*, was used as the exemplar to denote a maximal exogamous set – a set that also included Spider, Bluebird, and Carrying Strap ngyams – as well as a specific group within that set, should *Honngyam* be translated Bear "phratry" (for the exogamous set), Bear "clan" (the specific group), or Bear "lineage" (foregrounding the fact that it was composed of a group of blood-kin)?

To clarify the relationship between partner clans, it is important to distinguish between dispersed and localized clans. The localized clan, or village clan, is an organized, named, exogamic descent *group* in a particular village; while the dispersed clan is a named descent *category* found across several villages that is not organized (Aberle 1970; Bernardini 2005a:31–32). It is clear that Hopi migration traditions are intended to refer to the movements of a village clan, not a dispersed clan, because the latter is a category, not an organized unit.

The distribution of clan names across a landscape, however, is a result of processes involving *both* village clans and dispersed clans. The budding or fissioning of village clans could proliferate groups with related totems, for example Corn Root and Corn Husk from an original Corn clan (Parsons 1969:1067, n. 7; Titiev 1944:56–57). The migration of these groups would contribute to a dispersed clan system in which some similarly named village clans actually share a common heritage. At the same time, village clans in different villages will tend to adjust clan names to facilitate the extension of hospitality and marriage to distant groups, producing a dispersed clan system (Aberle 1970).

In sum, as Whiteley (2003) has argued, the terminological formalism of Titiev and Eggan in describing the household-lineage-clan-phratry series imposes discrete categories on what is actually a social continuum. Hopi descent groups employ variable markers and have incommensurate intensities of consolidation (Whiteley 2003:172) depending on the social context in which they are operating. While it is important to distinguish between village clans and dispersed clans to ensure that one is talking about an actual organized group, use of the term clan is best accompanied by an appreciation of the dynamism of the underlying group rather than by a rigid definition of it.

CLANS VS. CLAN SYMBOLS

Practical implications of the preceding discussion relate primarily to the interpretation of clan symbols. The fluidity of clan symbolism and the propensity for clan fissioning means that the presence of morphologically similar clan symbols in two different places, or at two different points in time, does not necessarily indicate the presence of the same group of people. Conversely, different, though typically thematically related, symbols can be used to mark the presence of the same group of people in two places or two points in time. When Hopi workmen employed by J.W. Fewkes signed for their paychecks, for example, different members of the same clan used different totems as their signatures (Fewkes 1897).

There is no easy answer to the question of how to read the presence of social groups from ancient clan symbol petroglyphs. In general, the freedom of a clan member to use multiple totems will have the effect of exaggerating the diversity of groups present at a given location. In the absence of detailed, diachronic ethnographic data, however, it will be difficult, if not impossible, to sort out totems being used as alternate symbols by a single group from totems intended to symbolize different groups. Indeed, as the discussion above indicates, two different members of the same group might simultaneously use symbols in both of these manners.

In the database of clan identifications compiled here, each morphologically distinct totem is labeled separately; that is, alternate symbols of a clan or phratry are not grouped together. Thus, even though Snake clan and Lizard clan members are free to use either snakes or lizards as their clan totem, by virtue of being partner clans, in this study a snake totem is classified as snake and a lizard totem is classified as lizard. When possible, however, the principal totem among the totems of partner clans, as recorded historically by Titiev (1944) and Edmund Nequatewa (Colton and Colton 1931:32–33), and as discussed during consultations with the Hopi CRATT (CRATT notes, August 18, 2005), is also listed. For example, the Water clan, or *Patkingyam* is understood to have at least two alternate totems, which are cloud and snow. A cloud symbol at Tutuveni would thus be classified in the database as cloud, with a principal totem as water. Principal totems are also listed for *Masaaw* (principal totem: fire), Germ God (principal totem: corn), and a series of katsinas – *Qööqöqlö*, *Soyàlkatsina*, Mud Head (principal totem: katsina). All tabulations reported in this book are counts of non-principal symbols.

CONCLUSION

Having clarified the nature of Hopi clans and their relation to clan symbols, the following chapter describes the field and lab recording procedures, and presents and analyzes the identified clan symbols at Tutuveni.

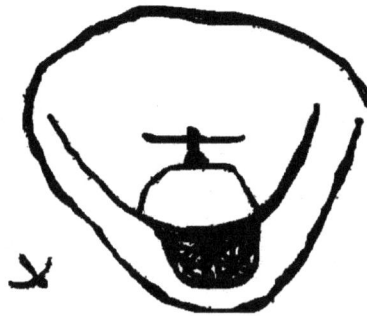

Chapter Three
Data and Analysis

Summary statistics for the Tutuveni petroglyphs reveal the magnitude of clan symbols concentrated there. The site contains 154 boulders with 235 separate panels, with 2,376 elements, or rows of images, which total 5,103 individual symbols. The purpose of this chapter is to explain how these data were collected and to conduct preliminary analyses to explore patterns of variability in them. The analyses presented here only scratch the surface of the data's research potential; therefore, future research directions are suggested at the conclusion of the chapter.

FIELD PROCEDURES

Documentation of the Tutuveni petroglyphs began with an aerial photograph of the site taken from a balloon-mounted digital camera (Fig. 3.1). The aerial photograph was geo-rectified in ArcMap 9.0, printed, and then used to trace boulder outlines and generate a map of the boulder field (Fig. 3.2). Boulders with petroglyphs were numbered sequentially along the lower terrace from north to south and on the hill-slope from south to north.

For the purposes of recording, each boulder was divided into one or more panels, or flat surfaces, which were labeled according to the direction the panel faces. Panels were labeled in the format "Boulder number, Panel." In the field, the first recording step was to fill out a form detailing each panel's dimensions, the presence of natural and cultural damage, and the details of the petroglyphs present (Fig. 3.3). Each panel was then photographed at five-megapixel resolution in its entirety with a metric scale. Then, close-up shots of individual elements or sections of the panel were taken. In all, 1,802 digital pictures were taken of the panels (DVD0001–DVD1802).

In the field, one or more of the overview photographs for each boulder face was printed on standard 8.5x11-inch paper using a portable color printer, and a transparency was placed over the print for tracing and note taking. The purpose of the in-field transparency drawings was not to trace every element, but rather to note details that were unclear in the photograph that might cause confusion in the lab. For example, elements in shadow or bright sun were highlighted, while elements covered by lichen or badly eroded were clarified. Several layers of transparencies were recorded for each boulder face (e.g., one layer to record petrolyph information, one layer to record vandalism, etc.).

LAB ANALYSIS

In the lab, a photograph of each boulder panel was enlarged, color and contrast were enhanced in Adobe Photoshop, and the image was printed on a color plotter at approximately a fifth of its original size, typically 24x36 in. Acetate sheets were then placed over the prints and

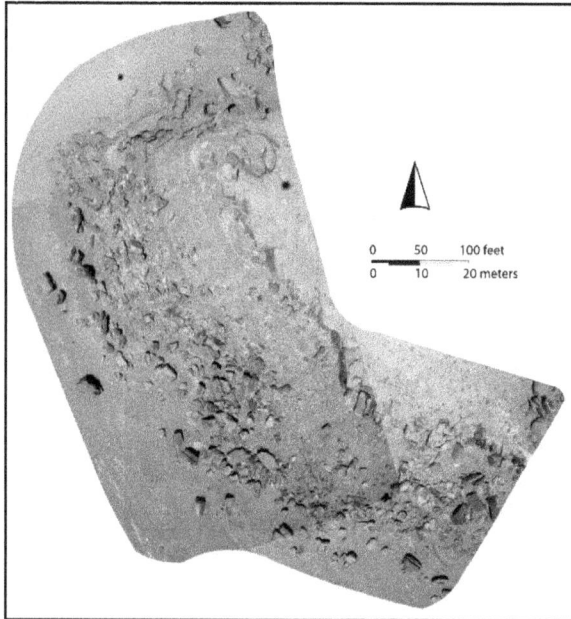

Figure 3.1. Aerial photograph of Tutuveni.

all visible petroglyphs were traced onto the acetate. To tabulate individual symbols, these line drawings were scanned and imported into CorelDraw 11.0. Using CorelDraw, each row of repeated symbols was designated as an element, outlined with a dashed-line box, and labeled with a capital letter or number (for example, a row of six corn symbols equals one element) (Fig. 3.4). Using the labeled line drawings, the number of different symbols present on each panel and the number of symbols within each element was then tabulated. These panel tables were compiled and entered into a master database, which is included on the DVD (Fig. 3.5).

Historical Photographs

In an effort to reconstruct the site in its pre-vandalized form and to establish the timing of damage to different boulders, a database of historical photographs of Tutuveni was compiled. Twelve sets of pictures spanning the period from 1930 to 2005 were assembled from the MNA, the UCLA Rock Art Archive, and several rock art researchers (Table 3.1),

totaling 766 photographs (a digital copy of each historical photograph is included on the DVD [DVD1803–DVD2564]). Each historical photograph was scanned and relabeled to correspond to the boulder numbering system used in the current project. The historical photographs enable researchers to work backwards to identify the original appearance of individual elements that have since been damaged or obliterated by vandalism. Table 3.2 lists the boulders and panels included in each of the historical photograph sets. Figure 3.6 shows the condition of a panel heavily affected by vandalism in its pre- and post-vandalism conditions (see Appendix I for more examples).

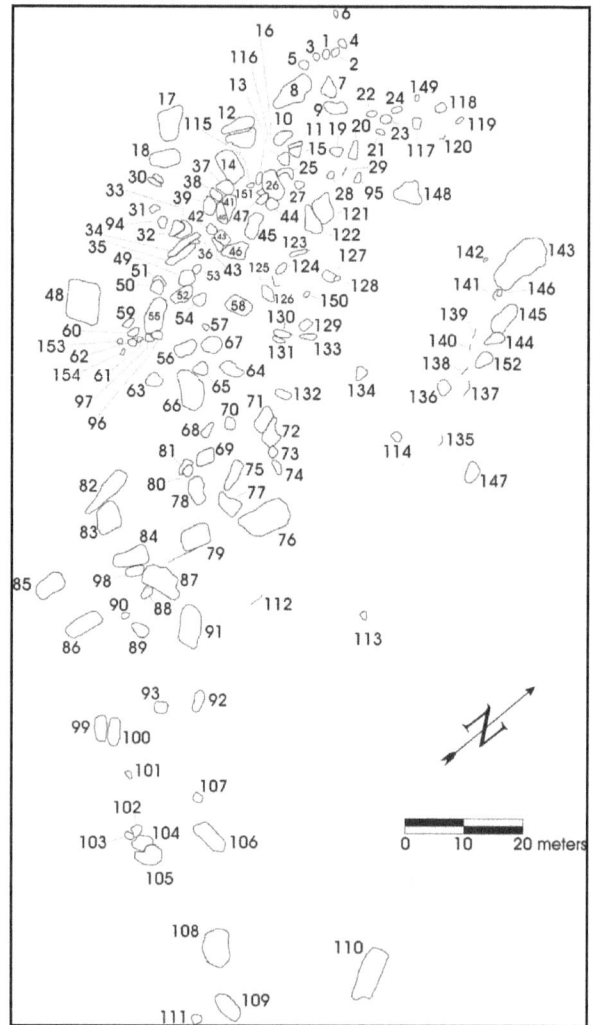

Figure 3.2. Numbered boulders at Tutuveni.

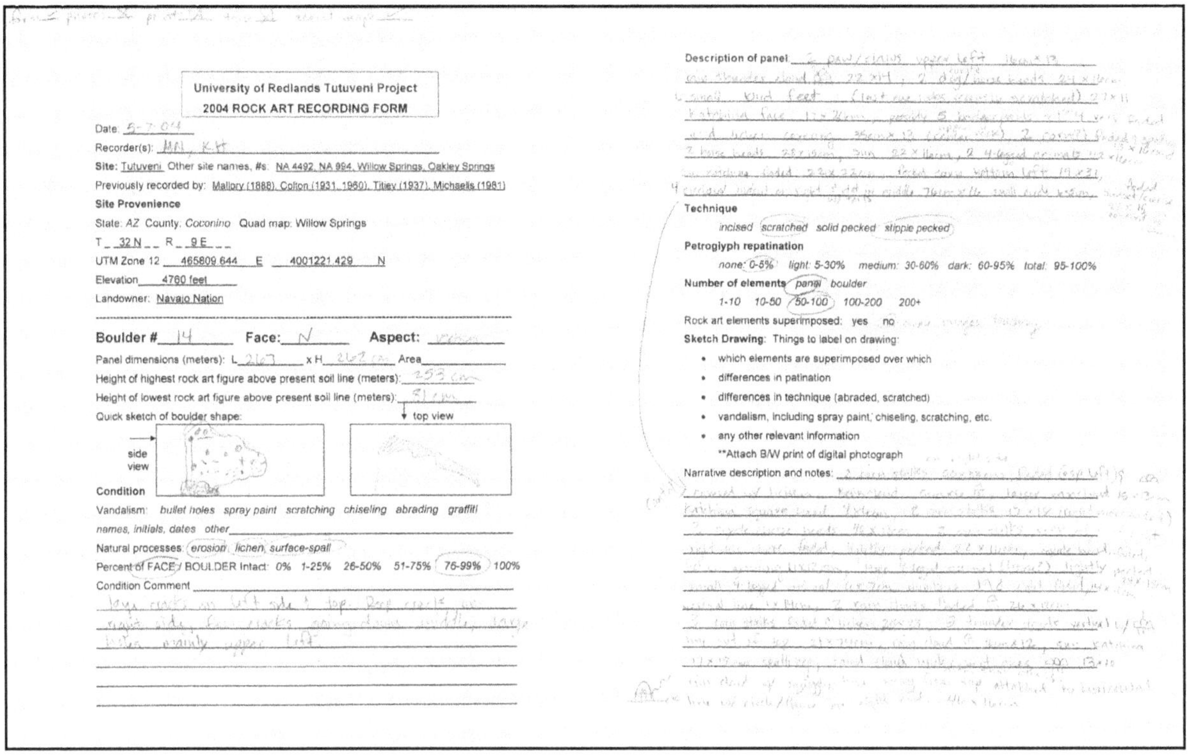
University of Redlands Tutuveni Project
2004 ROCK ART RECORDING FORM
Date: 5-7-04
Recorder(s): MN, KH
Site: Tutuveni Other site names, #s: NA 4492, NA 994, Willow Springs, Oakley Springs
Previously recorded by: Mallory (1888), Colton (1931, 1960), Titiev (1937), Michaelis (1981)
Site Provenience
State: AZ County: Coconino Quad map: Willow Springs
T 32 N R 9 E
UTM Zone 12 465809.644 E 4001221.429 N
Elevation 4760 feet
Landowner: Navajo Nation
Boulder # 14 Face: N Aspect:
Panel dimensions (meters): L x H Area
Height of highest rock art figure above present soil line (meters):
Height of lowest rock art figure above present soil line (meters):
Quick sketch of boulder shape: top view
side view
Condition
Vandalism: bullet holes spray paint scratching chiseling abrading graffiti
names, initials, dates other
Natural processes: erosion lichen surface-spall
Percent of FACE / BOULDER Intact: 0% 1-25% 26-50% 51-75% 76-99% 100%
Condition Comment

Description of panel
Technique
incised scratched solid pecked stipple pecked
Petroglyph repatination
none: 0-5% light: 5-30% medium: 30-60% dark: 60-95% total: 95-100%
Number of elements panel boulder
1-10 10-50 50-100 100-200 200+
Rock art elements superimposed: yes no
Sketch Drawing: Things to label on drawing:
- which elements are superimposed over which
- differences in patination
- differences in technique (abraded, scratched)
- vandalism, including spray paint, chiseling, scratching, etc.
- any other relevant information

**Attach B/W print of digital photograph
Narrative description and notes:

Figure 3.3. Sample boulder recording form, front and back.

Table 3.1. Sources of Historical Tutuveni Photographs.

Date of photographs	Institutional photo credit	Individual photo credit
1930	Cline Library, MNA	Harold Colton
1978	UCLA Rock Art Archives	Helen Michaelis
1981	-	Patricia McCreery
1984	-	Evelyn Billo & Robert Mark
1984	-	Donald Weaver
1989	-	Donald Weaver
1997	-	Donald Weaver
1998	-	Barbara Gronneman
1998	-	Evelyn Billo & Robert Mark
1999	-	Evelyn Billo & Robert Mark
2003	-	Wesley Bernardini
2004	University of Redlands	Wesley Bernardini
2005	University of Redlands	Wesley Bernardini

Line Drawings

The line drawings of each panel presented in this study reflect the pre-vandalism condition of petroglyphs whenever possible, although not all damaged elements could be reconstructed from the historical photograph database. Panels for which historical photographs were consulted to produce the line drawing are labeled in the caption as reconstructed; all others depict the panel condition in 2004. Panels were reconstructed back to the earliest available photograph(s),

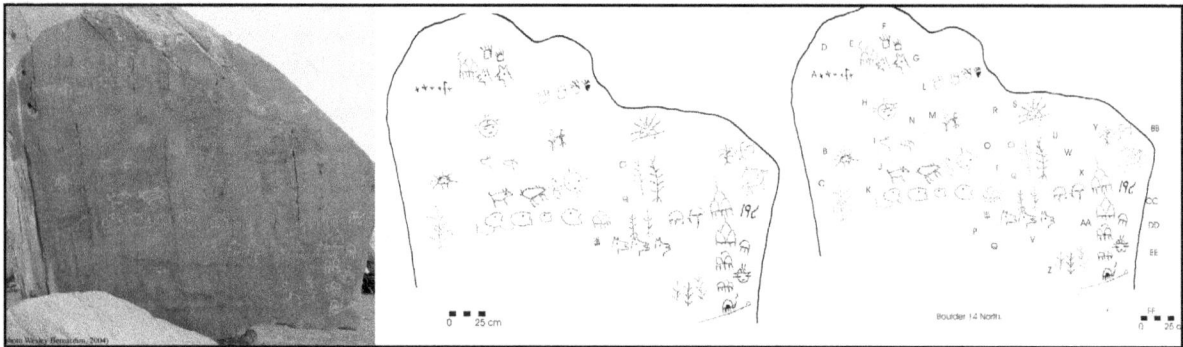

Figure 3.4. Example of element labeling.

	A	B	C	D	E	F	G	H	I
1	Boulder	Element	Clan Symbol	Principle Totem	# images	Defaced	Repatination	Technique	Comments
136	014_N	M	eagle		2	no	moderate	pecked	
137	014_N	N	unidentifiable		1	no	moderate	pecked	
138	014_N	O	sun		1	no	moderate	pecked	
139	014_N	P	katsina		1	no	moderate	pecked	
140	014_N	Q	water		1	no	moderate	pecked	
141	014_N	R	cloud	water	1	no	moderate	pecked	
142	014_N	S	sun forehead		1	no	moderate	pecked	
143	014_N	U	corn		4	no	moderate	pecked	
144	014_N	V	coyote		3	no	light	pecked	
145	014_N	X	water		8	no	moderate	pecked	repatination and style vary in row
146	014_N	Y	corn		3	no	moderate	pecked	
147	014_N	Z	corn		3	no	light	pecked	
148	014_S	A	modern symbol		1	no	light	scratched	human figure
149	014_S	AA	water		1	no	moderate	pecked	lightning
150	014_S	B	coyote		1	no	moderate	pecked	
151	014_S	BB	unidentifiable		1	no	light	scratched	
152	014_S	C	corn		10	no	moderate	pecked	
153	014_S	CC	unidentifiable		1	no	light	scratched	
154	014_S	D	bear/badger		4	no	moderate	pecked	
155	014_S	DD	corn		1	no	moderate	pecked	
156	014_S	E	parrot		3	no	moderate	pecked	
157	014_S	EE	Máasaw	Fire	5	no	heavy	pecked	style changes in row
158	014_S	F	unid. bird		3	no	moderate	pecked	
159	014_S	FF	corn		4	no	moderate	pecked	
160	014_S	G	bear/badger		4	no	moderate	pecked	
161	014_S	GG	corn		5	no	heavy	pecked	Germ God is one of 5
162	014_S	I	coyote		2	no	light	pecked	
163	014_S	II	katsina		1	no	moderate	pecked	one-horn katsina
164	014_S	J	sun forehead		1	no	moderate	scratched	
165	014_S	JJ	unid. bird		1	no	moderate	pecked	
166	014_S	K	bow		2	no	light	pecked	
167	014_S	KK	Máasaw	Fire	2	no	moderate	pecked	
168	014_S	L	katsina		2	no	moderate	pecked	possible mudhead
169	014_S	M	horn		1	no	moderate	pecked	
170	014_S	MM	bear/badger		5	no	moderate	pecked	
171	014_S	N	unid. bird		1	no	light	pecked	3-toed
172	014_S	NN	Germ God	corn	1	no	moderate	pecked	
173	014_S	P	Máasaw	Fire	5	no	moderate	pecked	
174	014_S	Q	corn		5	no	moderate	pecked	
175	014_S	R	bear/badger		7	no	moderate	pecked	
176	014_S	S	unidentifiable		1	no	light	scratched	scratched line
177	014_S	T	corn		1	no	moderate	scratched	
									possible parrot; symbol on left has

| ◄ ◄ ► ►|\ **Sheet1** / Sheet2 / Sheet3 / | | |◄| |

Figure 3.5. Sample page from the Tutuveni database.

Table 3.2. Boulders and Panels Included in the Historical Photograph Sets.

Panel	1930 Colton	1978 Michaelis	1981 McCreery	1984 Billo-Marks	1984 Weaver	1989 Weaver	1997 Weaver	1998 Gronneman	1998 Billo-Marks	1999 Billo-Marks	2003 Bernardini	2004 Bernardini
1 SE												X
2 TOP												X
3 TOP												X
4 W												X
5 S												X
5 N												X
5 W												X
6 S												X
7 S												X
7 SW												X
8 S												X
8 W	X	X	X	X	X	X		X	X	X	X	X
8 SE										X		X
9 SE		X	X						X	X		X
10 W				X					X	X		X
11 W												X
12 SW		X	X	X		X				X	X	X
12 E	X			X	X					X	X	X
13 NW										X		X
13 W												X
13 T												X
13 SW									X	X		X
13 NE									X	X		X
14 N	X	X				X		X		X		X
14 S	X	X			X	X	X	X	X	X	X	X
14 E	X			X							X	X
15 T												X

Table 3.2. Boulders and Panels Included in the Historical Photograph Sets, cont'd.

Panel	1930 Colton	1978 Michaelis	1981 McCreery	1984 Billo-Marks	1984 Weaver	1989 Weaver	1997 Weaver	1998 Gronneman	1998 Billo-Marks	1999 Billo-Marks	2003 Bernardini	2004 Bernardini
16 E	X											X
17 NW			X	X	X				X	X		X
17 T												X
17 SE	X	X		X					X	X	X	X
17 NE												X
17 S	X	X	X	X	X		X	X	X	X		X
18 T	X			X	X			X	X	X		X
18 T(W)												X
18 N	X								X	X		X
18 S	X	X	X							X		X
18 W	X	X	X	X	X			X	X	X		X
18 SW	X									X		X
19 NW												X
20 SW			X	X	X					X		X
21 SE												X
22 E												X
23 S		X										X
24 NE												X
25 T												X
26 W												X
27 S												X
28 S				X						X		X
29 SW												X
30 T												X
30 S	X	X	X	X	X	X		X	X	X	X	X
30 N									X	X		X
31 E												X

Table 3.2. Boulders and Panels Included in the Historical Photograph Sets, cont'd.

Panel	1930 Colton	1978 Michaelis	1981 McCreery	1984 Billo-Marks	1984 Weaver	1989 Weaver	1997 Weaver	1998 Gronneman	1998 Billo-Marks	1999 Billo-Marks	2003 Bernardini	2004 Bernardini
32 SW												X
32 B												X
33 N		X								X		X
33 T												X
34 T		X	X	X	X				X	X		X
34 S		X	X							X		X
34 N		X			X							X
34 W				X					X	X		X
34 E												X
35 NE												X
35 T	X		X			X			X	X	X	X
35 W												X
35 E												X
35 S		X	X							X	X	X
36 E	X	X	X						X	X		X
37 T	X	X	X	X	X		X		X	X	X	X
38 S												X
38 SW												X
39 N												X
39 T												X
40 S										X		X
40 E	X	X	X	X	X					X		X
41 T												X
42 T												X
43 S	X	X	X	X	X		X		X	X	X	X
44 T												X
45 NW												X

Table 3.2. Boulders and Panels Included in the Historical Photograph Sets, cont'd.

Panel	1930 Colton	1978 Michaelis	1981 McCreery	1984 Billo-Marks	1984 Weaver	1989 Weaver	1997 Weaver	1998 Gronneman	1998 Billo-Marks	1999 Billo-Marks	2003 Bernardini	2004 Bernardini
45 T		X		X	X					X	X	X
46 W		X		X						X	X	X
46 SW									X			X
47 S												X
48 SE	X	X	X	X	X			X		X	X	X
48 NE	X		X	X							X	X
48 NE TOP SHELF												
48 N SHELF N												X
48 NW	X	X		X					X			X
48 SW	X	X	X		X			X	X	X	X	X
48 T				X								X
49 NW					X				X			X
49 NE										X		X
49 SW	X	X							X	X	X	X
49 SE												X
50 T									X	X		X
50 W				X								X
50 SW						X						X
51 NW												X
51 B								X				X
52 T		X			X				X	X		X
52 W			X	X					X	X		X
52 E												X

Table 3.2. Boulders and Panels Included in the Historical Photograph Sets, cont'd.

Panel	1930 Colton	1978 Michaelis	1981 McCreery	1984 Billo-Marks	1984 Weaver	1989 Weaver	1997 Weaver	1998 Gronneman	1998 Billo-Marks	1999 Billo-Marks	2003 Bernardini	2004 Bernardini
52 S												X
53 SE												X
53 T										X	X	X
54 S		X									X	X
55 NE									X	X		X
55 N												X
55 W	X	X			X				X	X	X	X
55 S										X	X	X
55 T												X
56 T		X								X		X
56 SE												X
57 SE												X
58 T			X							X	X	X
59 W												X
60 T		X		X	X				X	X	X	X
60 S		X								X	X	X
60 SW												X
60 W									X	X	X	X
61 S												X
61 NW					X							X
61 SW												X
62 T												X
63 T												X
64 S											X	X
64 T		X								X		X
65 E												X
66 SE												X

Table 3.2. Boulders and Panels Included in the Historical Photograph Sets, cont'd.

Panel	1930 Colton	1978 Michaelis	1981 McCreery	1984 Billo-Marks	1984 Weaver	1989 Weaver	1997 Weaver	1998 Gronneman	1998 Billo-Marks	1999 Billo-Marks	2003 Bernardini	2004 Bernardini
66 S												X
66 NW												X
66 E												X
67 E												X
68 T												X
69 W												X
70 T												X
71 T												X
72 W				X								X
72 SE										X	X	X
73 T												X
74 SW												X
75 W		X	X	X					X	X		X
76 W		X		X							X	X
77 S										X		X
78 SW												X
79 SW			X									X
80 W												X
81 T												X
82 W		X	X	X					X	X		X
83 SW												X
83 SE										X		X
84 T												X
85 SW			X									X
85 NW												
85 SE												X
86 E												X

Table 3.2. Boulders and Panels Included in the Historical Photograph Sets, cont'd.

Panel	1930 Colton	1978 Michaelis	1981 McCreery	1984 Billo-Marks	1984 Weaver	1989 Weaver	1997 Weaver	1998 Gronneman	1998 Billo-Marks	1999 Billo-Marks	2003 Bernardini	2004 Bernardini
87 W												X
87 T												X
88 T												X
89 N												X
89 T												X
90 NE												X
91 E												X
92 W												X
93 T												X
94 SW			X							X		X
95 T											X	X
96 SE											X	X
97 SE												X
98 T												X
99 SW												X
99 SE												X
100 NE												X
101 T												X
102 SW												X
103 SW												X
104 NW												X
105 S												X
105 E												X
106 SW												X
107 T												X
108 S												X
108 E												X

Table 3.2. Boulders and Panels Included in the Historical Photograph Sets, cont'd.

Panel	1930 Colton	1978 Michaelis	1981 McCreery	1984 Billo-Marks	1984 Weaver	1989 Weaver	1997 Weaver	1998 Gronneman	1998 Billo-Marks	1999 Billo-Marks	2003 Bernardini	2004 Bernardini
109 N												X
109 S												X
110 T												X
111 T												X
112 W												X
113 S												X
114 NW												X
115 NW		X										X
116 SW												X
117 T												X
118 T												X
119 W												X
120 NW												X
121 SE												X
122 W											X	X
122 SE												X
123 NW												X
124 W												X
125 SW												X
126 SW	X				X					X		X
127 T												X
128 W												X
129 W												X
130 T					X					X		X
131 T					X					X		X
132 T												X
133 SE												X

Table 3.2. Boulders and Panels Included in the Historical Photograph Sets, cont'd.

Panel	1930 Colton	1978 Michaelis	1981 McCreery	1984 Billo-Marks	1984 Weaver	1989 Weaver	1997 Weaver	1998 Gronneman	1998 Billo-Marks	1999 Billo-Marks	2003 Bernardini	2004 Bernardini
134 T												X
135 SW												X
136 SW												X
137 W										X		X
137 SW										X	X	X
138 NW												X
139 SW												X
140 SW												X
141 NW												X
142 T												X
143 T												X
143 NW												X
143 SW												X
144 T												X
145 T												X
146 NW												X
147 T												X
148 T												X
149 T												X
150 T												X
151 NW												
152 T									X			
153 T									X	X		
154 SW										X		

a 1930 photograph by Harold Colton (copyright Museum of Northern Arizona; DVD1811).

b. 2004 photograph by Wesley Bernardini (DVD0329).

Figure 3.6., I.18. Boulder 17 Northwest .

which is usually either 1930 or 1978, as these are the two most comprehensive sets of historical images. The repatination column in Fig. 3.5 also records the pre-vandalism repatination whenever it was possible to observe this.

The resulting line drawings of all 235 panels are included on the DVD (DVD2565–DVD3050) and each panel is presented once unlabeled and once labeled, for a total of 488 drawings. Some panels were so large that they were drawn in quarters, thirds, or halves. The labeled line drawings permit other researchers to independently tabulate symbols. An example of a line drawing of a panel with significant numbers of clan symbols is illustrated in Figure 3.7 (additional line drawings appear in Appendix I).

IDENTIFYING CLAN SYMBOLS

Petroglyph elements were initially identified and named based on information provided to anthropologists by Hopi cultural advisors at four different points over the past 120 years. The two earliest sources of information are publications by Jesse Walter Fewkes (1892, 1897). In the first source, Fewkes (1892) consulted a number of unnamed Walpi inhabitants for assistance in interpreting petroglyphs on First Mesa, including a number of clan symbols. The second Fewkes (1897) publication is perhaps the most valuable historical source, as it contains a collection of clan symbols used as signatures by Hopi workmen in the late nineteenth century. Fewkes documented 24 clan symbols produced by 116 Hopi men, each of whom provided a verbal interpretation of his signature.

A third source of information is found in Harold and Mary Colton's (1931) account of a visit to Tutuveni with Hopi advisor Edmund Nequatewa. Nequatewa was a member of the Sun Forehead clan from Second Mesa. Although he was an initiated, and therefore knowledgeable, Hopi man, because he was not from Third Mesa, he did not have an insider's view of Tutuveni and of the clans that used the site most frequently. Thus, although Nequatewa's identifications of clan symbols are likely accurate, they are not necessarily comprehensive. Nequatewa suggested that symbols he did not recognize might be extinct clans, an interpretation seconded by current Hopi CRATT members (Notes from CRATT meeting, August 18, 2005).

A fourth source is an article by Helen Michaelis (1981) summarizing her documentation of the Tutuveni site. During her site visits several unnamed Hopi consultants accompanied her and helped interpret petroglyphs. Michaelis' field identifications, combined with her review of Nequatewa's clan list published

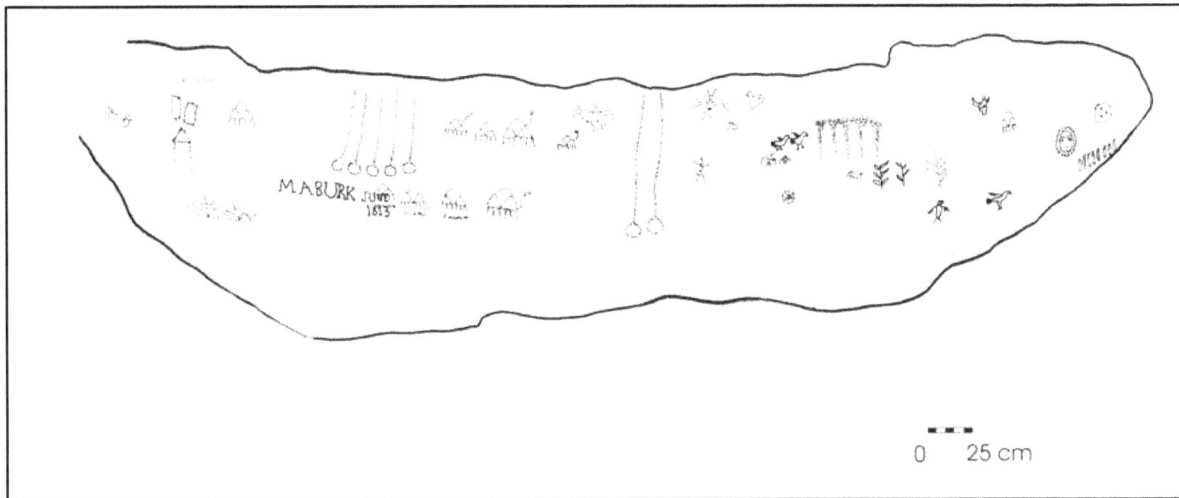

Figure 3.7, I.91. Boulder 8 west (reconstructed using 1930 photographs).

in Colton and Colton (1931), resulted in the documentation of 40 Hopi clan symbols at Tutuveni.

For the current project, the clan symbols identified by all four sets of Hopi cultural advisors were compiled into a single reference sheet that was used to make preliminary identifications of the Tutuveni elements. These preliminary identifications were then presented to a Hopi CRATT meeting on August 18, 2005 for confirmation and clarification. A paper survey form, including copies of line drawings of all major panels, was also circulated to representatives of the 11 occupied Hopi villages. The participants in these consultations are listed in Table 3.3. The identifications of symbols across all five independent consultations with Hopi advisors over 120 years are remarkably consistent (Table 3.4). Especially encouraging is the correspondence between totemic petroglyphs at Tutuveni and the hand-drawn totemic signatures of Hopi workmen recorded by Fewkes (1897) (Figure 3.8), as these symbols were produced to symbolize clan identity in two completely different cultural contexts.

This process resulted in the identification of 76 totemic symbols, including several different categories. Thirty-two symbols corresponded to the marks of living or recently extinct clans

(Fig. 3.9); six symbols corresponded to katsinas still active in Hopi ritual (Fig. 3.10); and 38 symbols, which occurred repeatedly but did not correspond to any current or recently extinct Hopi clan, were interpreted as symbols of extinct clans (Fig. 3.11). Images were classified as extinct clan symbols if they had clear iconography and occurred multiple times either in a row or in different places, but did not correspond to any historically documented Hopi totem. Each of these symbols was assigned a number (for example, Extinct-1, Extinct-2, etc.). The vast majority of these extinct clan symbols are found on boulder 48, the oldest rock at Tutuveni based on repatination. The assemblage of extinct clan symbols is discussed in further detail below.

Three additional categories were used for elements that could not be linked to a historically recorded clan symbol. The Unknown category was used for elements that appeared to be representations of a recognizable object, such as a plant, but which did not contain sufficient distinguishing characteristics for a definitive identification. The unknown category was comprised primarily of three groups: unknown birds, unknown plants, and unknown quadrupeds (Fig. 3.12). The Unique category was used for elements that had clear iconography, but

Table 3.3. Hopi Advisors Consulted During the Tutuveni Project.

Hopi Participants	Village	Clan	August 18, 2005 CRATT meeting	Village Survey Form
Clay Hamilton	Sitsomovi	Deer	X	
Clayton Honyumptewa	Lower Munqapi	Snake	X	
Dalton Taylor	Songòopavi	Sun	X	
Frank Honahnie, Sr.	Kiqötsmovi/Munqapi	Coyote	X	X
Gilbert Naseyouma	Munqapi	Sun	X	X
Harlan Williams	Musangnuvi	Eagle	X	
Harold Polingyumptewa	Hotvela	Sand	X	X
LaVern Siweumptewa	Musangnuvi	Water	X	
Lee Wayne Lomayestewa	Songòopavi	Bear	X	
Leigh Kuwanwisiwma	Paaqavi	Greasewood	X	
Marvin Lalo	Walpi	Tobacco/Rabbit	X	
Morgan Saufkie	Songòopavi	Bear	X	
Owen Numkena, Jr.	Musangnuvi	Corn	X	X
Raleigh Puhayaoma, Sr.	Supawlavi	Sun Forehead	X	X
Stewart Koyiyumptewa	Hotvela	Badger	X	
Sue Kuyvaya	Songòopavi	Water/Fog	X	
Valjean Joshevama	Songòopavi	Sun	X	
Walter Hamana	Old Orayvi	Greasewood	X	
Wilton Kooyahoema	Hotvela	Fire	X	

Clan symbol	Tutuveni petroglyphs	Totemic signatures
Lizard		
Bear		
Snake		
Water/ Cloud		
Sun		
Rabbit		
Corn		

Figure 3.8. Examples of clan symbols from Tutuveni (left) and Fewkes' (1897) list of Hopi totemic signatures.

Table 3.4. Clan Symbols Identified by Hopi Consultants.

Clan Symbol	Fewkes 1897	Fewkes 1892	Forde 1931	Colton 1931	Michaelis 1981	2005 CRATT meeting
Arrow						X
Badger				X		X
Bear	X		X	X	X	X
Bear Strap				X		X
Bluebird				X		
Bow				X		X
Butterfly	X			X	X	X
Cactus	X					
Cloud				X		X
Corn	X	X	X	X	X	X
Coyote	X			X	X	X
Deer	X					
Eagle				X		X
Fire						X
Greasewood						X
Horn				X		X
Katsina	X	X	X	X	X	X
Lizard	X		X	X	X	X
Máasaw (Fire)						X
Moon				X		
Mud Head Katsina						X
Oak				X	X	
Parrot				X		X
Qööqöqlö Katsina						X
Rabbit				X		X
Red Ant				X		
Reed				X		
Sand				X		X
Snake	X	X	X	X	X	X
Snow						X
Soyoko Katsina						X
Spider				X		X
Squash	X					X
Sun						X
Sun Forehead				X		X
Tobacco	X				X	
Water						X

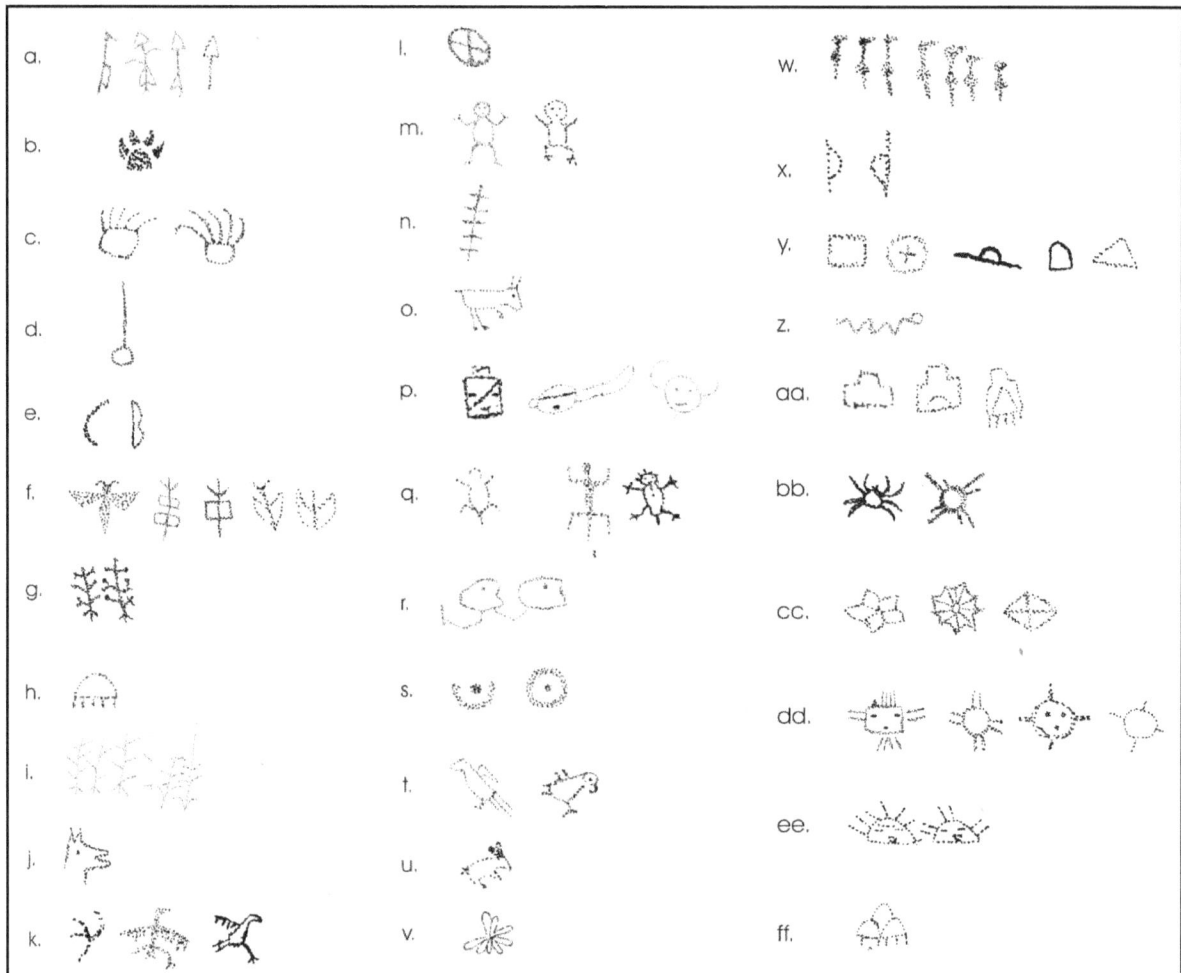

Figure 3.9. Clan symbols of living or recently extinct Hopi clans observed at Tutuveni. a. arrow, b. badger, c. bear, d. bear strap, e. bow, f. butterfly, g. cactus, h. cloud (water), i. corn, j. coyote, k. eagle, l. fire, m. germ god (corn), n. greasewood, o. horn, p. katsina, q. lizard, r. Máasaw (Fire), s. moon, t. parrot, u. rabbit, v. rabbit brush, w. red ant, x. reed, y. sand, z. snake, aa. snow (water), bb. spider, cc. squash, dd. sun, ee. sun forehead, ff. water.

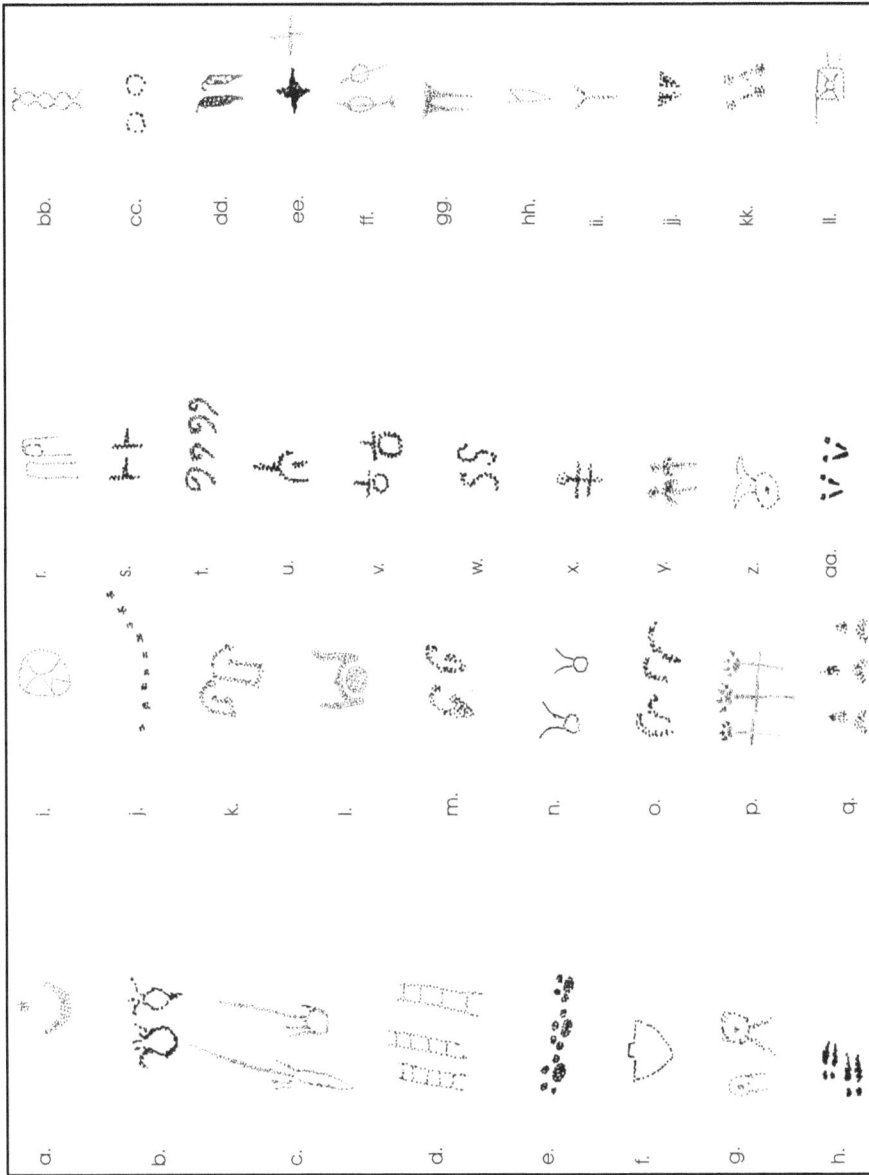

Figure 3.11. *Symbols of extinct clans at Tutuveni. a. Extinct-1, b. Extinct-2, c. Extinct-3, d. Extinct-4, e. Extinct-5, f. Extinct-6, g. Extinct-7, h. Extinct 8, i. Extinct-9, j. Extinct-10, k. Extinct-11, l. Extinct-12, m. Extinct -13, n. Extinct-14, o. Extinct-15, p. Extinct-16, q. Extinct-17, r. Extinct-18, s. Extinct-19, t. Extinct-20, u. Extinct-21, v. Extinct-22, w. Extinct-23, x. Extinct-24, y. Extinct-25, z. Extinct-26, aa. Extinct-27, bb. Extinct-28, cc. Extinct-29, dd. Extinct-30, ee. Extinct-31, ff. Extinct-32, gg. Extinct-33, hh. Extinct-34, ii. Extinct-35, jj. Extinct-36, kk. Extinct-37, ll. Extinct-38.*

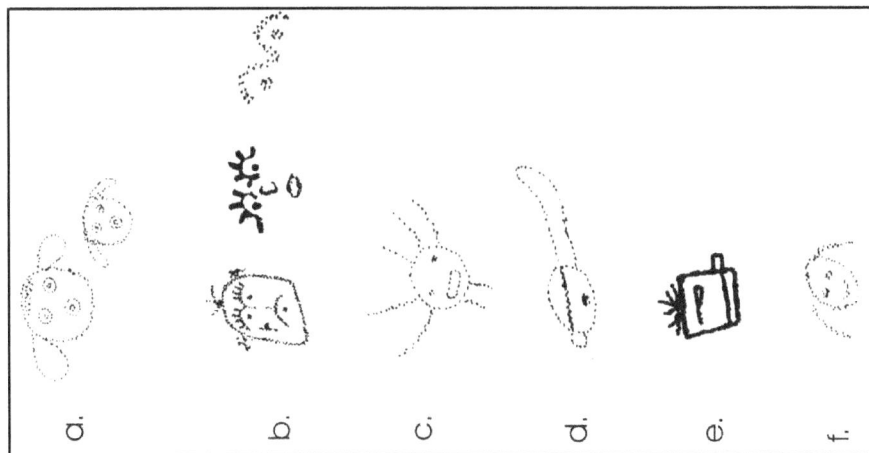

Figure 3.10. *Katsina symbols at Tutuveni that correspond to historical Katsinas. a. Mud Head Ogre (Colton 1959:28), b. Qööqölö (Colton 1959:21), c. Soyal, d. Wupa'-ala (Colton 1959:42), e. Áhooli (Colton 1959:2), f. an unnamed katsina associated with the Wuwtsim society.*

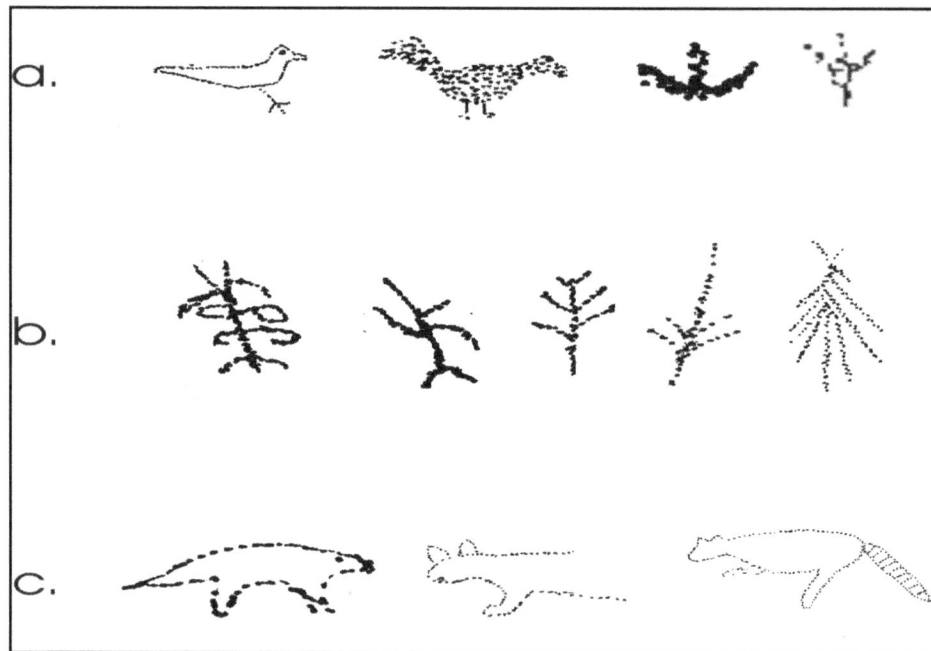

Figure 3.12. Examples of unknown symbols at Tutuveni. a. unknown birds, b. unknown plants, c. unknown quadrupeds.

occurred only once at the site (Fig. 3.13). These were labeled with a number, such as Unique-1. The Unidentifiable category was used for elements that were visually unintelligible, such as images that were badly faded or eroded.

A number of symbol categories require clarification to make the criteria for their classification explicit:

• Bear and Badger are separately named Hopi clans in different phratries, and although Hopi consultants indicated that bear and badger paws should be distinguishable by the number of fingers depicted (five vs. four or three, respectively [CRATT meeting, August 18, 2005]), this variable proved inadequate to discriminate the paw symbols. After many attempts to separate bear paws from badger paws, they were eventually lumped into a single bear/badger category, despite the fact that this combines two currently distinct clans.

• The Unknown Bird category sub-

sumes considerable variability in form and style, probably encompassing at least five different living or recently extinct Hopi bird clans, including Bluebird, Crow, Crane/Heron, Pigeon-Hawk (Colton and Colton 1931:34–35), and perhaps several additional ones. Unfortunately, neither morphology nor input from Hopi cultural advisors was sufficient to consistently separate most bird symbols into discrete categories.

• Distinguishing corn symbols from other plants proved difficult, and it is likely that some of the symbols grouped under the category corn could be separated into sub-classes of plants. The horizontal leaves of greasewood symbols, for example, grade into the curved leaves of corn. The totems of the Young Corn and Corn clans (see Table 2.1) are also indistinguishable with the current information.

• Sun and Sun Forehead symbols of-

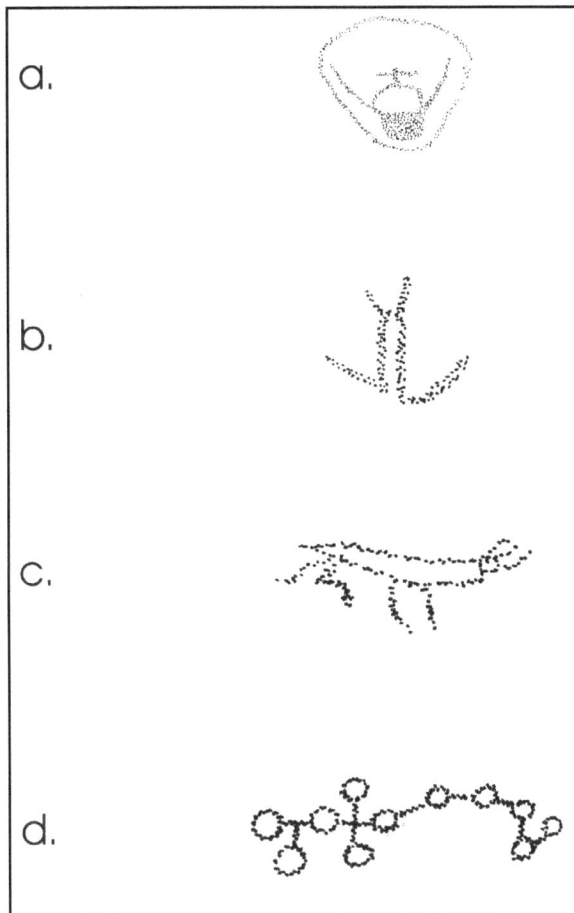

Figure 3.13. Unique symbols at Tutuveni. a. Unique-1 (boulder 48 southeast element 73), b. Unique-2 (boulder 30 south element KK), c. Unique-3 (boulder 30 south element NN), d. Unique-4 (boulder 48 southwest element 76).

ten occurred on the same row (e.g., 18 North element C, 17 Northwest element L), suggesting that they may have been used as alternate totems at Tutuveni.

• Snake and Lizard symbols occasionally occurred on the same row, suggesting that they may have been used as alternate totems at Tutuveni. This is clearly demonstrated in 33 Top element H.

• Water, Cloud, and Snow symbols were separated by Hopi cultural advisors at the 2005 consultation, but these symbols occasionally occurred on the same row (e.g., 14 North element AA),

suggesting that they may have been used as alternate totems at Tutuveni.

• Hopi cultural advisors consulted in 2005 revised two of Edmund Nequatewa's symbol identifications made in 1931, concluding that Nequatewa had mistakenly identified a butterfly symbol as a red ant, and several arrow symbols as reeds (Colton and Colton 1931:Figure 2; Fig. 3.9, this volume). In both of these cases, the present study deferred to the identifications of the 2005 assembly of cultural advisors given the breadth of the traditional knowledge they brought to the process.

• A large number of katsina images were identified at Tutuveni, but the majority proved difficult to correlate with historically recorded katsinas or dolls; therefore, most of these are lumped under a general Katsina category. The Katsina category almost certainly encompasses a number of distinct symbols, potentially of distinct clans (see below).

PATTERNS AND ANALYSIS

Of the 5,103 symbols at Tutuveni, the vast majority (4,283 or 84 percent) are intelligible glyphs. The remaining marks are English graffiti, or are too faint, eroded, or poorly executed to be interpreted. All further statistics presented in this chapter were generated from study of the 4,283 intelligible glyphs (excluding the categories "English writing" and "unidentifiable"). Sixty percent (2,537) of the symbols are found on boulder 48, the largest, most centrally located, and most heavily repatinated boulder on the site. Of the remaining images, most (24 percent) are found on seven boulders which cluster around boulder 48, which include boulders 8, 14, 17, 18, 30, 34, and 55 (Fig. 3.14). The remaining symbols are scattered among

144 other boulders, most of which contain fewer than six glyphs each.

Symbol Frequency

The symbols at Tutuveni are dominated by three very common images: Bear/Badger paws, Unknown-birds, and Corn (Table 3.5, Fig. 3.15). Together, these three categories comprise 23 percent of the total symbols at Tutuveni. These "Class A" symbols are common in large part because they are all composite categories, encompassing a diversity of symbols that potentially refer to multiple clans. If all katsina images are grouped together, including Katsina, Sun, Sun Forehead, *Qööqöqlö*, Mud Head, and *Soyàlkatsina*, they represent the fourth most common symbol, with 312 images. Closer examination of the rest of the frequency distribution suggests the existence of five additional frequency categories: Class B (165–210 symbols); Class C (90–120 symbols); Class D (40–62 symbols), and Class E (20–30 symbols); and Class F (11 or fewer symbols) (Figure 3.16; Table 3.6).

Symbol frequency at Tutuveni is a product of clan size and clan longevity. In an effort to identify unusually large and/or long-lived clans, symbol frequency was quantified using Z-scores. Z-scores express the deviation of a quantity from the mean of a distribution in terms of numbers of standard deviations (Shennan 1997:75). For example, a Z-score of two indicates that the observed value is two standard deviations greater than the mean. In a normally distributed population, only 16 percent of the values would deviate from the mean by more than one standard deviation, and only 2.5 percent would deviate by more than two standard deviations. Thus, Z-scores provide a basis for identifying outlying cases that are substantially different from the rest of the sample.

For a given set of observations, Z-scores

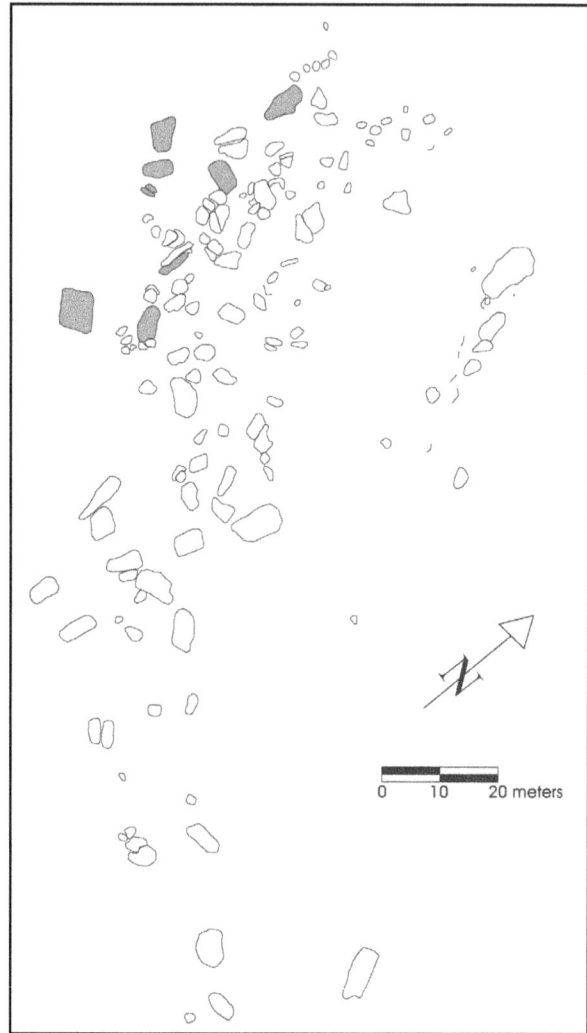

Figure 3.14. Primary boulders at Tutuveni.

are calculated by subtracting the mean from the observed value and dividing the results by the standard deviation. In order to calculate Z-scores at Tutuveni, each symbol's mean percentage of occurrence across the entire site was subtracted from its observed percentage on a particular boulder panel, and the result was divided by the standard deviation for that symbol across the entire site. Table 3.7 displays the Z-scores for 28 large boulder panels at Tutuveni. To simplify the display, Z-scores of 1.0–1.99 are represented by a +, and Z-scores of 2.0 or greater are represented by a ++. The table reveals a complex pattern in which every symbol except one, Extinct-20, is unusually

Table 3.5. Tutuveni Petroglyph Symbols by Frequency.		
Clan Symbol	Number of Elements	Total Number of Symbols
Bear/Badger	215	587
Unknown-Bird	205	576
Corn	192	473
Unidentifiable	329	457
English Writing	350	363
Coyote	74	208
Lizard	77	208
Sun	87	188
Extinct-10	27	166
Máasaw	38	120
Cloud	44	119
Snake	53	113
Unknown	70	113
Bow	30	109
Water	50	102
Snow	37	91
Bear Strap	25	90
Butterfly	32	62
Katsina	44	60
Parrot	30	60
Sand	24	56
Red Ant	16	51
Arrow	15	47
Modern Symbol	32	45
Eagle	22	42
Extinct-30	10	41
Rabbit	13	40
Germ God	11	30
Extinct-31	14	28
Horn	14	28
Squash	10	28
Qööqöqlö Katsina	13	27
Spider	5	27
Sun Forehead	15	26
Extinct-20	3	25
Unknown-Plant	20	25
Extinct-05	10	23
Reed	9	23
Extinct-18	2	11
Extinct-32	8	11
Greasewood	9	11
Mud Head Katsina	3	11
Extinct-29	6	10

Table 3.5. Tutuveni Petroglyph Symbols by Frequency, cont'd.		
Clan Symbol	Number of Elements	Total Number of Symbols
Extinct-33	2	10
Extinct-16	2	8
Extinct-34	2	8
Moon	5	8
Extinct-17	3	8
Extinct-22	1	7
Unknown-Quadruped	7	7
Extinct-04	4	6
Extinct-06	5	6
Extinct-27	1	6
Extinct-28	2	6
Fire	3	6
Oak	2	6
Cactus	4	5
Extinct-02	3	4
Extinct-14	3	4
Extinct-15	1	4
Extinct-23	1	4
Extinct-35	3	5
Extinct-37	1	4
Extinct-03	2	3
Extinct-09	3	3
Extinct-11	1	3
Extinct-12	2	3
Extinct-21	2	3
Extinct-25	1	3
Extinct-36	1	3
Extinct-38	1	3
Badger	1	2
Extinct-01	1	2
Extinct-07	1	2
Extinct-08	1	2
Extinct-13	1	2
Extinct-26	1	1
Rabbitbrush	1	1
Soyàlkatsina	1	1
Unique-1	1	1
Unique-2	1	1
Unique-3	1	1
Unique-4	1	1
Total	2375	5103

abundant on at least one panel. This pattern suggests that most clans are locally abundant on at least one boulder face, and that clan symbols do not regularly cluster together.

Spatial Patterns
Further exploration of relationships among clan symbols using cluster analysis (Ward's

method and Average Linkage, run on squared Euclidean distance of the Z-score data) suggests several clusters of panels with similar sets of images. This includes six panels with unusually abundant sun, unidentified bird, corn, and bear symbols (48 Northeast, 48 Top, 48 Southwest, 35 West, 48 Northwest, and 48 Southeast); three panels with *Máasaw* and

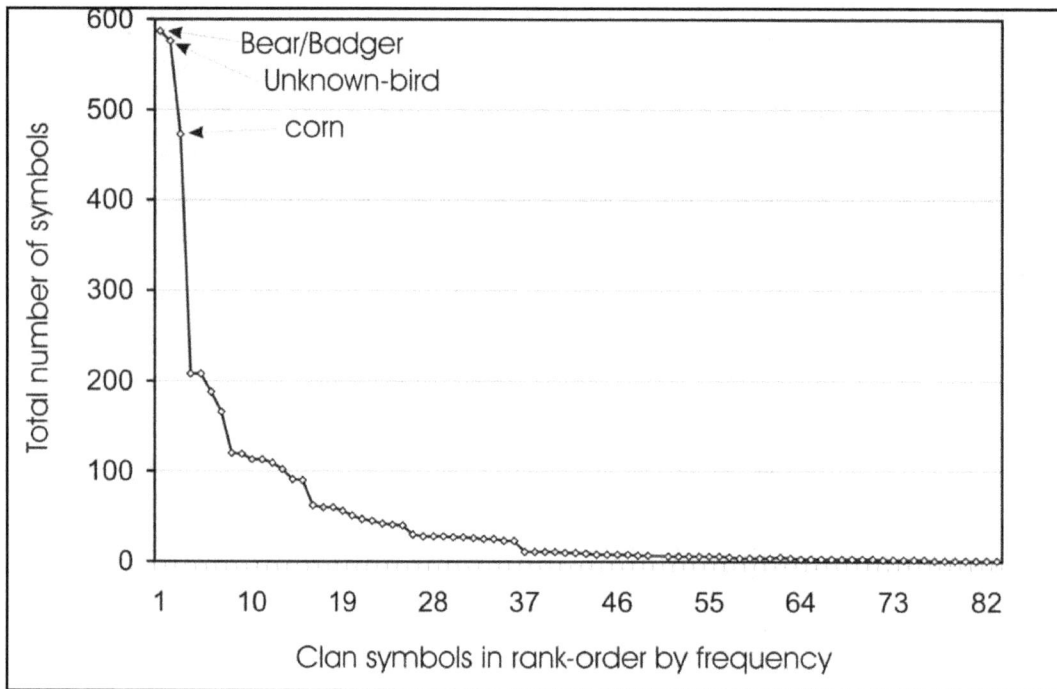

Figure 3.15. Symbol frequency at Tutuveni.

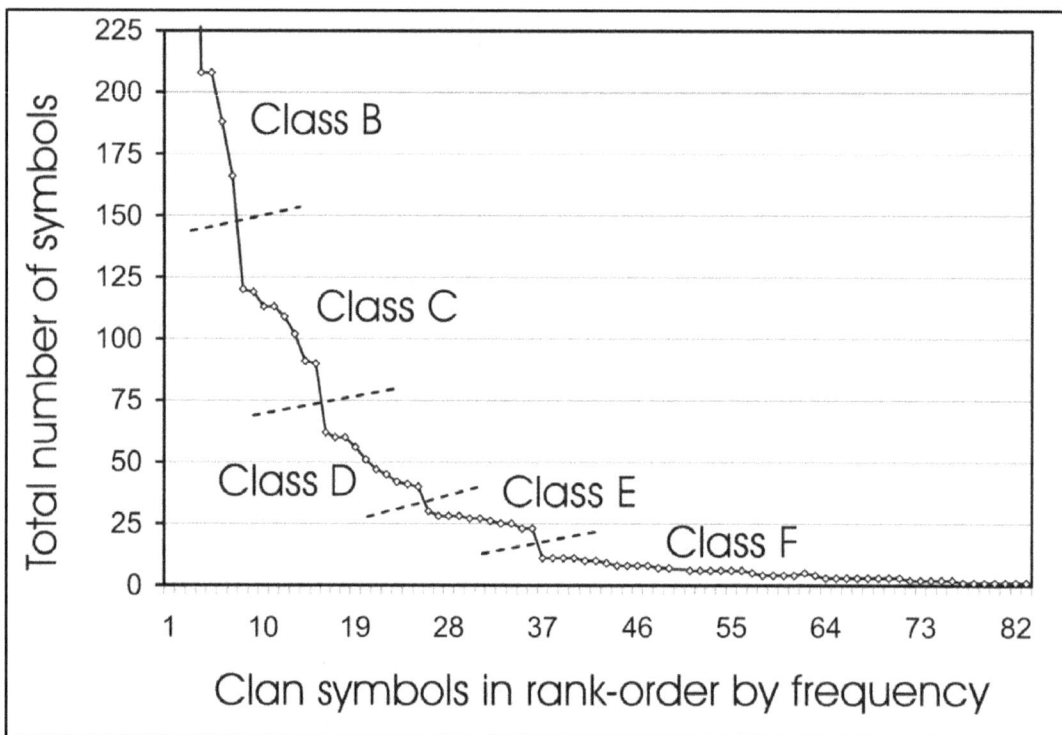

Figure 3.16. Symbol frequency at Tutuveni, Class B – Class F.

Table 3.6. Symbols Arranged by Frequency Class.		Table 3.6. Symbols Arranged by Frequency Class, cont'd.	
Class	Symbol	Class	Symbol
Class A	Bear/Badger	Class F	Extinct-18
	Unknown-Bird		Extinct-32
	Corn		Greasewood
	Katsina (combined)		Mud Head Katsina
			Extinct-29
Class B	Coyote		Extinct-33
	Lizard		Extinct-19
	Sun		Extinct-16
	Extinct-10		Extinct-34
			Moon
Class C	*Máasaw*		Extinct-17
	Cloud		Extinct-22
	Snake		Unknown-Quadruped
	Bow		Extinct-04
	Water		Extinct-06
	Snow		Extinct-27
	Bear Strap		Extinct-28
			Fire
Class D	Butterfly		Oak
	Katsina		Cactus
	Parrot		Extinct-02
	Sand		Extinct-14
	Red Ant		Extinct-15
	Arrow		Extinct-23
	Eagle		Extinct-35
	Extinct-30		Extinct-37
	Rabbit		Extinct-03
			Extinct-09
Class E	Germ God		Extinct-11
	Extinct-31		Extinct-12
	Horn		Extinct-21
	Squash		Extinct-25
	Qööqöqlö Katsina		Extinct-36
	Spider		Extinct-38
	Sun Forehead		Badger
	Extinct-20		Extinct-01
	Unknown-Plant		Extinct-07
	Extinct-05		Extinct-08
	Reed		Extinct-13
			Extinct-26
			Rabbitbrush
			Soyàlkatsina
			Unique-1
			Unique-2
			Unique-3
			Unique-4

snake symbols (33 Top, 49 Southwest, and 35 Top); three panels with corn, sun forehead, and water symbols (14 North, 18 Southwest, and 8 West); and three panels with cloud, coyote, squash, and sun symbols (18 Top, 18 West, and 17 Northwest). All of these panels are in the northwest corner, or old, section of the site (Fig. 1.5), and within this relatively small area none form particularly discrete spatial clusters. All of the clusters combine symbols of clans currently housed in different phratries (Table 3.1) and clans of diverse ceremonial

Table 3.7. Relative Abundance of Clan Symbols Based on Z-score Transformation of Symbol Percentages.

Symbol	35 T	35 W	37 T	43 S	48 NE	48 NW	48 SE	48 SW	48 T	49 SW	50 T	55 W	60 T	82 W
Arrow							+							
Bear/Badger		+	++					+	++					+
Bear Strap											++			++
Bow							+							
Butterfly				++				++						
Cloud														
Corn		++				+	+		+					
Coyote	++	+												
Eagle				++							++			
Extinct-05			++											
Extinct-10							++	++						
Extinct-20														
Extinct-30														
Extinct-31						++				++				
Germ God	++	++								++				
Horn					+									
Katsina				++		++						++		
Lizard			+			+	++							++
Máasaw											++	++		
Parrot	+													
Qööqöqlö	++		++											
Rabbit			++									++	+	
Red ant	++					+								
Reed														
Sand		+										++		
Snake	++					+				++				
Snow								++	+					
Spider													++	
Squash														
Sun					++				++					
Sun Forehead														++
Unknown-Bird					+	++			+					
Water	+			++		+							+	

Table 3.7. Relative Abundance of Clan Symbols Based on Z-score Transformation of Symbol Percentages, cont'd.

Symbol	8 W	13 NE	14 N	14 S	17 NW	17 S	17 SE	18 S	18 SW	18 T	18 W	30 S	33 T	34 T
Arrow														
Bear/Badger								++	+				++	
Bear Strap	++			++	++		+						+	
Bow										++		+		
Butterfly														
Cloud		+							++	++	++	+		
Corn			++	++		++			++	++		++		
Coyote		+	++		++		++			++	++			
Eagle			+				++							
Extinct-05										++				
Extinct-10														
Extinct-20														
Extinct-30	++						++							
Extinct-31														
Germ God														
Horn			++			+						+	+	
Katsina	++	++		+										
Lizard		+				++	++							
Máasaw			+	++			+			++			++	
Parrot	++						+							+
Qööqöqlö														
Rabbit														
Red ant														
Reed														
Sand	++	+						+						
Snake							++						++	++
Snow														
Spider														
Squash	+				++		++				++			
Sun		++			++	++					++			
Sun Forehead	++	++	++				+	+						
Unknown-Bird		++							+		+	+		
Water	++		++		++	+			++					++

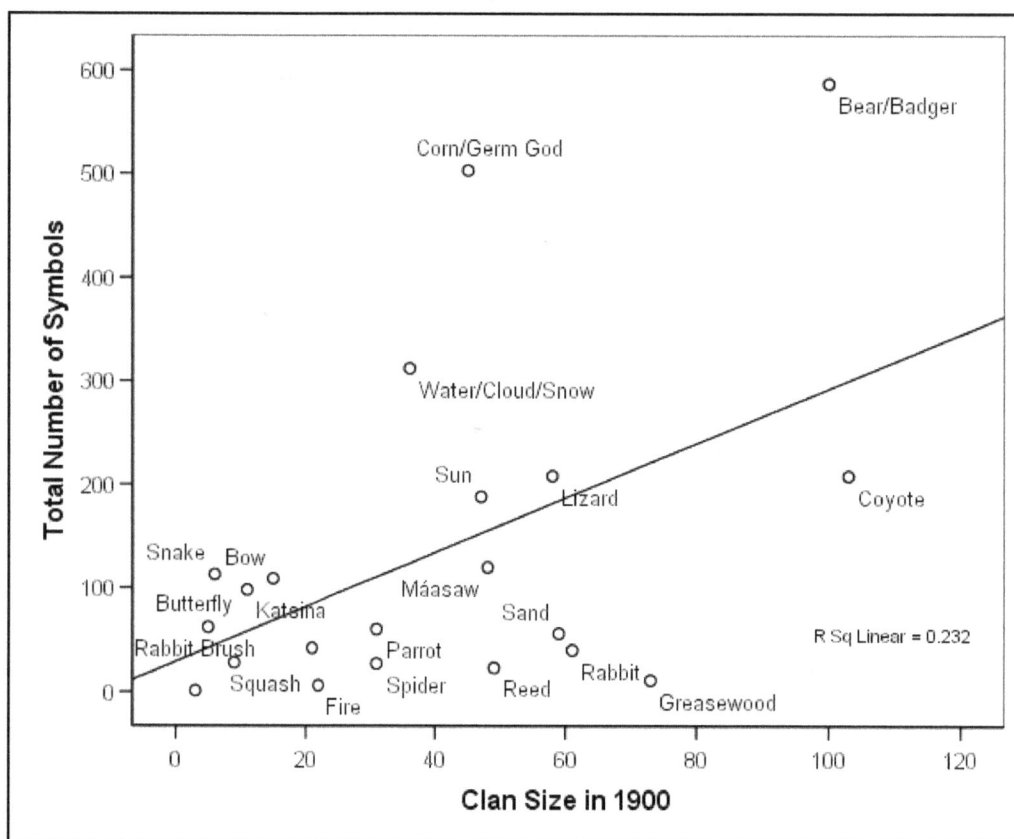

Figure 3.17. Plot of clan size in 1900 (data from Titiev 1944:Chart VI) vs. symbol frequency at Tutuveni.

ranks (Levy 1992: Table 3.1). Further spatial analysis might reveal additional patterns, or suggest additional meaning for those identified here, but this preliminary analysis indicates that clans did not concentrate their symbols together. Instead, each panel appears to reflect the diversity of each class of *Wuwtsim* initiates who traveled to Tutuveni together on a given year's salt pilgrimage.

Symbol Frequency and Clan Population
Clan symbol frequency correlates only weakly with clan population in Orayvi in 1900 (Titiev 1944:Chart VI [note that several totems are combined to match the clans observed at Orayvi, such as Water/Cloud/Snow]) ($r^2 = 0.23$; see Fig. 3.17). That is, the symbols of the more populous Orayvi clans of the early 1900s tend to be somewhat more common at Tutuveni than

are the symbols of smaller clans, but about 77 percent of the variation in symbol frequency is unexplained by clan size in 1900. Given the long history of use of Tutuveni by Hopi clans, the use of Tutuveni by multiple villages and mesas, and the high rate of demographic turnover likely suffered by small social groups (Gaines and Gaines 1997), it is unsurprising that population size at one village during one recent moment in time is a poor predictor of overall symbol frequency.

Symbol Frequency and Clan Rank
Symbol frequency also shows no correlation ($r^2 = 0.07$; Fig. 3.18) with a clan's early twentieth-century ceremonial and land ownership ranking, as compiled by Levy (1992:41) for Orayvi in 1900. That is, the symbols of higher-ranking clans are not more frequently

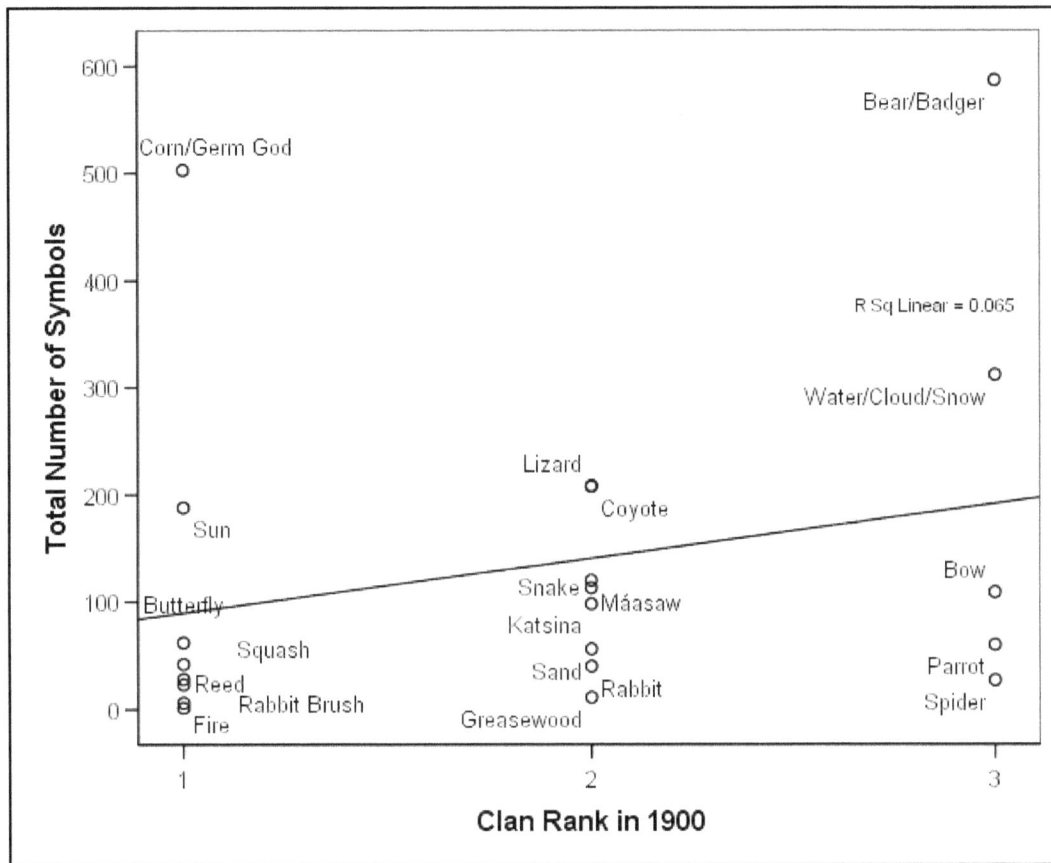

Figure 3.18. Plot of clan rank in 1900 (data from Levy 1992:Table 3.1) vs. symbol frequency at Tutuveni.

represented at Tutuveni than the symbols of lower-ranking clans. While this is again unsurprising given that clan status likely shifted over the centuries of visitation at Tutuveni, the lack of any patterning in the relationship of these two variables confirms that participation in the *Wuwtsim* initiation was not limited to clans of certain ceremonial status. This accords with ethnographic accounts of the *Wuwtsim* as the pan-tribal initiation ceremony through which most Hopi boys passed into adulthood (Titiev 1944:136). Also supporting an interpretation of relatively democratic access to the Salt Trail pilgrimage among Hopi clans is the fact that the clan symbols of the leaders of the salt pilgrimage are present but not unusually abundant at Tutuveni (compare Eggan 1950:94-95 to Fig. 3.18).

Number of Visits Per Clan

As recorded ethnographically and in Hopi traditional knowledge, the pilgrimage along the Salt Trail was a regular event, ideally held every four years. Each visit produced one clan signature for each member of the pilgrimage. Repeated visits by the same individual or by members of the same clan produced lines of the same symbol, representing the number of consecutive trips made to the site. Interestingly, symbols were placed to the left of previous signatures (Titiev 1937:245–246). Analysis of the number of symbols in a row is therefore a measure of the longevity of different clans.

Table 3.8 presents a list of symbols ranked by the number of times they are found in a given row. As can be seen, the vast majority of rows are short, with a mean of 2.1 and a standard deviation of 2.2 symbols in a row. Some symbols, however, occur in very long rows, suggesting regular visitation by a populous and stable clan. The longest row, at 27 symbols, which represents 27 visits, is comprised of unknown bird symbols, which cannot be linked to a specific historical clan. Other symbols found in unusually long rows include *Máasaw*, Lizard, Cloud, Corn, Bear/Badger, Bow, and Extinct-20, all of which are found in rows of 15–21 symbols. If the *Wuwtsim* initiation was held every four to sixteen years in the past, as it was in the historical period, members of these clans participated in pilgrimages for stretches of 60–330 years. The members of these long-lived, active clans must have been prominent in the political structure of Third Mesa Hopi villages. In fact, Bow, Bear, and Water Clans were among the most powerful Hopi clans in the early twentieth century, and *Máasaw* and Lizard were second-level clans (Levy 1992:Table 3.1). Future research could compare symbol frequency at Tutuveni to other lines of evidence from residential sites, measuring clan size, longevity, and status.

Extinct Clans

During a 1930 visit to Tutuveni by Harold and Mary Colton, Hopi consultant Edmund Nequatewa identified several symbols of recently extinct clans (Colton and Colton 1931:32). His identifications were subsequently confirmed by contemporary Hopi consultants (August 18, 2005 CRATT meeting). In fact, 38 different types of symbols, comprising 447 images, conform to the style and size that characterize contemporary clan symbols at Tutuveni, and appear alongside known clan symbols in similar, repeated rows (Fig. 3.11), strongly suggesting that these icons were used to symbolize the group identities of

now extinct clans (tentative identifications by current Hopi Cultural Preservation Office staff include: Extinct-1, *Muyaw* [Moon]; Extinct-5, coyote; Extinct-8, deer; Extinct-16, coyote; Extinct-24, *Holi* [Butterfly]; Extinct-25, parrot; Extinct-27, deer/rabbit; Extinct-30, corn; and Extinct-31, star). The term *extinct* is somewhat problematic given the discussion of clans and clan totems in Chapter 2, because alternate totems can be latent for long periods of time before being reactivated to link individuals or groups together. Nevertheless, it is clear that some totems have passed out of use, whether through the actual extinction of group members or through decline in social status of the symbol.

The large number of extinct clan symbols at Tutuveni testifies to the time depth of Hopi use of the site. If we assume that the rate of clan extinction observed in the historical period has been constant through time, we can estimate the age of Tutuveni from the number of extinct clans. This is an admittedly questionable assumption, given the concentration of epidemic disease outbreaks in the post-contact period; nevertheless, it is a potentially useful heuristic one. Two historical-era censuses of the village of Orayvi, one by Stephen in 1891 and one by Titiev in 1932, provide the data to estimate a rate of clan extinction over time. There are three clans listed by Stephen as present in 1891 that were not counted by Titiev in 1931 (*Kwan*, Moth, and Burrowing Owl); however, Titiev (1944:55) emphasizes that most such discrepancies are due to differences in nomenclature, with only *Kwan* qualifying as a possible instance of clan extinction. If we take a range of 1–4 clan extinctions over the period from 1891–1931 (equivalent to 2.5–10 extinctions per century) and apply this range to the 38 extinct clan symbols at Tutuveni, we may infer an age of 380–1500 years for the site.

Working in the opposite direction, given that ceramics, repatination and petroglyph style

Table 3.8. Symbols Arranged by Maximum Row Length.

Clan Symbol	Maximum Row length
Unknown-Bird	27
Máasaw	21
Lizard	20
Cloud	19
Corn	18
Bear/Badger	16
Bow	15
Extinct-20	15
Bear Strap	12
Extinct-10	12
Germ God	12
Spider	12
Arrow	11
Coyote	11
Extinct-30	11
Sun	11
Parrot	10
Red Ant	8
Reed	8
Water	8
Extinct-19	7
Extinct-22	7
Sand	7
Snow	7
Squash	7
Butterfly	6
Eagle	6
Extinct-18	6
Extinct-27	6
Extinct-34	6
Katsina	6
Qööqöqlö Katsina	6
Rabbit	6
Snake	6
Extinct-05	5
Extinct-16	5
Extinct-28	5
Extinct-31	5
Extinct-33	5
Sun Forehead	5
Extinct-15	4

Table 3.8. Symbols Arranged by Maximum Row Length, cont'd.

Clan Symbol	Maximum Row length
Extinct-17	4
Extinct-23	4
Extinct-37	4
Fire	4
Horn	4
Mud Head Katsina	4
Oak	4
Extinct-04	3
Extinct-11	3
Extinct-25	3
Extinct-29	3
Extinct-32	3
Extinct-35	3
Extinct-36	3
Extinct-38	3
Moon	3
Unknown-Plant	3
Badger	2
Cactus	2
Extinct-01	2
Extinct-02	2
Extinct-03	2
Extinct-06	2
Extinct-07	2
Extinct-08	2
Extinct-12	2
Extinct-13	2
Extinct-14	2
Extinct-21	2
Greasewood	2
Extinct-09	1
Extinct-26	1
Rabbitbrush	1
Soyàlkatsina	1
Unique-1	1
Unique-2	1
Unique-3	1
Unique-4	1
Unknown-Quadruped	1

indicate an age for Tutuveni of perhaps 500 years, we may infer that an average of 7.5 clans from Hopi villages, or 12 percent of the 62 clans listed in Table 2.1, must have gone extinct every century, suggesting considerable dynamism or turnover in the labels used to identify groups, if not in the actual groups themselves. Simulations of small group survival rates produce comparable figures, demonstrating that up to 47 percent of 10-person groups may die out within three human generations simply due to stochastic fertility and mortality factors (Gaines and Gaines 1997).

KATSINAS

Katsinas are spirit beings who visit Hopi villages in the form of rain and clouds. Ceremonies involving katsinas have been observed as a part of Pueblo ritual since the time of Spanish contact (Hammond and Rey 1928:79). Katsina iconography, found on both petroglyphs and ceramics, appears first in the archaeological record of northern Arizona around A.D. 1250 to 1325 (Adams 1991). The collection of 312 katsina petroglyphs at Tutuveni is by far the largest concentration recorded at any site in the American Southwest.

The relationship between individual katsinas and particular clans is of special concern to the present study. Eggan (1950:91) noted that the Katsina clan controls the major opening and closing katsina ceremonies in each Hopi village; however, the control of the katsina rituals during the rest of the season was more complex. During the "open" katsina season anyone can ask the village chief's permission to sponsor a dance, and new katsinas may be introduced to the village. Each katsina ceremony is theoretically sponsored by a clan, but membership in the kiva groups that perform the dances is drawn from multiple clans (Eggan 1994:13). There is, however, one important exceptional category of katsinas. The exception is *mong*, or chief, katsinas, each of which is associated with just one clan (Titiev 1944:109).

The totemic signatures recorded by Fewkes (1897) suggest a complex relationship between clan and katsina in contemporary Hopi society, because workmen who self-identified as Katsina clan members signed with a variety of katsina totems, including Mud Head, *Hehey'a*, Navajo, and *Áhooli* katsinas. As the discussion in Chapter 2 made clear, it is difficult to determine whether these different katsina images, which include both *mong* and common katsinas, are intended to signify sub-groups within a larger unit, or simply alternative symbols of the same social unit.

Plog and Solometo (1997) hypothesize an earlier, one-to-one relationship between katsinas and clans, and suggest that that the modern Hopi ritual cycle evolved as a way of binding these diverse groups into an integrated whole. Supporting this hypothesis is the fact that the longer rows of katsinas at Tutuveni tend to contain a single, repeated katsina face, rather than mixing various faces in a row. Rows with three or more identical katsinas include sets of Sun, Sun Forehead, *Qööqöqlö*, and

Mud Head katsinas. Because these rows of symbols are homogenous, the symbols could be interpreted as totems of a particular social unit in which katsina image and clan totem are isomorphic. Of these images, however, only the Sun (*Taawa*), katsina today is a *mong* katsina associated with a particular clan.

Seventy-one percent of the katsina symbols at Tutuveni occur in isolation, which is a substantially higher proportion than symbols in the total population (46 percent). While many of these isolated symbols may simply be records of a single visit by a member of the Katsina clan, the high frequency of isolated katsina images suggests that not all may have been produced to symbolize clan identity. Several katsinas identified at Tutuveni play important roles in major katsina ceremonies and the depiction of these katsinas at Tutuveni may have been intended to symbolize broader ritual concepts, rather than clan identity *per se*. The *Soyàlkatsina*, for example, wears *Wuwtsim*-related objects and has the honor of opening the katsina season (Titiev 1944:110). The *Áhooli* katsina is involved in the Solstice and Bean Dance ceremonies. The *Kwaakwant* and *Aa'alt* societies that are part of the *Wuwtsim* initiations are known as the One-Horn and Two-Horn societies, respectively, and the one-horned and two-horned katsinas depicted at Tutuveni could represent these societies.

NON-CLAN SYMBOLS

The presence of several unique symbols (Fig. 3.18), which do not correspond to the conventions of the majority of symbols at Tutuveni, suggest that, like some katsina images, they may not be clan symbols. In addition to their relative isolation on the panel, these unique symbols also tend to be two or three times larger than the average symbol. Furthermore, their subject matter is distinctive. For example, Unique-1 depicts a katsina-like image inside a larger circle, situated prominently high in the center of the southeast panel of boulder 48. Unique-2 and Unique-3 are closely spaced, oversized images amidst a cluster of conventional clan symbols on the south panel of boulder 30, the latter apparently an insect of some sort. Unique-4 is a series of circles conjoined by lines, stretching for nearly a meter across the middle of boulder 48 southwest. Patricia McCreery notes that a petroglyph closely resembling Unique-4 has also been observed at the Boundary site in the Petrified Forest. Consultations with Hopi cultural advisors produced no information on these unique symbols.

CONCLUSION

Presentation and preliminary analysis of the Tutuveni petroglyphs demonstrates the incredible potential of this material for research into Puebloan identity. One of the most promising avenues of future inquiry at Tutuveni may be in-depth spatial analyses of symbols across the site. Spatial statistics such as K-means (Kintigh and Ammerman 1982) and a variety of cluster-analysis techniques could be used to identify clusters of co-occurring symbols. Clusters might be inferred to reflect partner clans, clans of similar status, or contemporaneous clans. Comparing patterns of frequency and spatial distribution of the Tutuveni petroglpyphs to other lines of evidence that reflect relationships among social groups from Hopi villages would also likely be very rewarding.

Chapter Four
Vandalism

Damage to the petroglyphs at Tutuveni has been lamented by researchers since the 1970s. The author of the 1986 National Register of Historic Places nomination form noted that:

> Names, dates, bogus clan signs, and a variety of graffiti have been added in recent years. Several of these later inscriptions were scratched or painted across Hopi panels, esthetically damaging but not obliterating them. The continuing vandalism of the site is the primary reason for the urgency of this nomination, as a first step towards other actions to protect this valuable resource (Tessman 1986:4).

Systematic documentation of vandalism at Tutuveni for the current study recorded significant damage to, or obliteration of, 222 elements, comprising 431 symbols, or roughly 10 percent of the intelligible symbols at the site. The number of damaged symbols does not include scratched or spray-painted graffiti applied indiscriminately to an entire boulder face, which effectively damages all nearby symbols (Fig. 4.1). In all, 51 boulder faces have been damaged (22 percent of the total panels at the site) including most of the central boulders containing the oldest clan symbols.

The chronological range of graffiti on boulders at Tutuveni attests to the length of time over which people have visited and damaged the site. The earliest dated graffiti is from 1872; while the most recent is from 2005. Figures 4.2 and 4.3 illustrate that although Tutuveni has suffered vandalism throughout the last 120 years, the pace of damage has increased significantly in the last two decades. Almost 80 percent of the datable vandalism at Tutuveni occurred between 1980 and 2004. Of particular concern is the appearance of potentially gang related graffiti noted on the author's most recent site visit in May of 2005 (Fig. 4.4). This design was inscribed using a motorized drill, carving deep into the surface of Boulder 48. The appearance of gang graffiti is alarming because, as with spray-painted signatures in urban areas, one signature tends to attract others. If motorized drills continue to be used for these signatures, Tutuveni will quickly become irrecoverably scarred.

OBLITERATED SYMBOLS

Although many boulders have been damaged by indiscriminate scratching, spray-painting, and carved initials, some symbols have been specifically targeted for damage (Fig. 4.5). In these cases, a particular symbol was selected from among dozens or hundreds on a boulder face and then completely obliterated using either pecking or chiseling. Obliteration is a distinctly different type of damage than casual graffiti, both in its motivation and effect. It is also distinct from the renovation of petroglyphs documented at some other sites (Cheremisin 2002; Hedges 1990), in which elements are

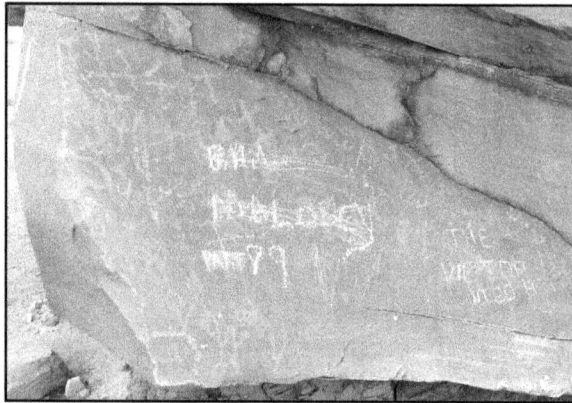

Figure 4.1. Detail of northwest face of Boulder 48, showing graffiti damage; DVD0952.

187	2333
188	
189	
190	6
191	
192	
193	01
194	348
195	000056778
196	15569
197	0223
198	223344445567889
199	011334678899999
200	00000122444

Figure 4.2. Stem and leaf diagram of graffiti dates at Tutuveni.

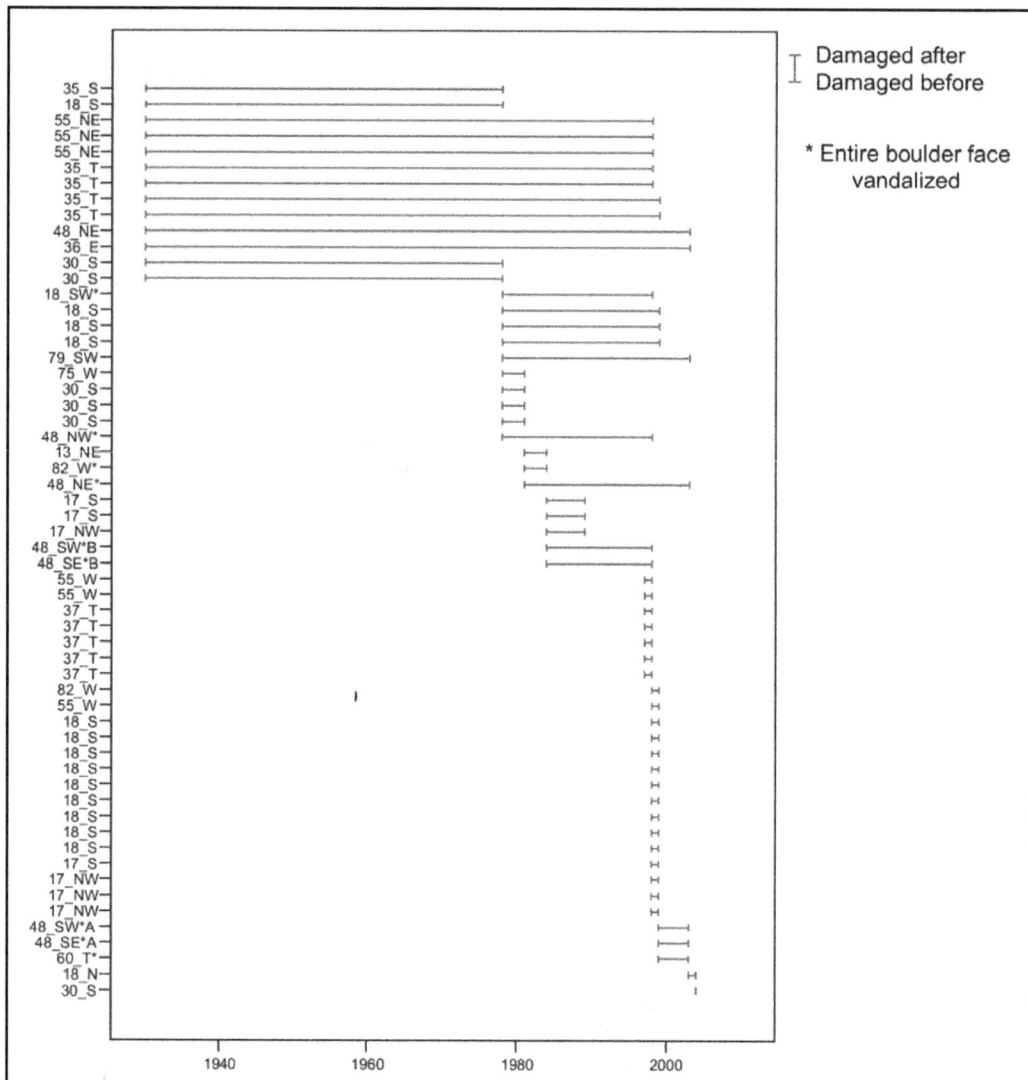

Figure 4.3. Damage to symbols over time at Tutuveni (all datable vandalism plotted).

Figure 4.4. Graffiti recorded in May 2005, Boulder 48, Northwest panel; DVD2559.

repecked or new elements are added to existing panels by descendant communities. In contrast to casual vandalism or renovation, the obliteration of elements at Tutuveni is specifically intended to remove an element or

elements from view. The targeted obliteration of particular symbols suggests that the vandal attributed a specific meaning to the chosen symbol and wished not just to damage it, but to erase it entirely.

To recover these obliterated images, historical photographs were consulted to identify pictures of symbols before the obliteration occurred. A total of 109 obliterated symbols, located on 28 different panels, were documented at Tutuveni, of which 88 symbols could be reconstructed from historical photographs. Tabulation of the obliterated symbols reveals interesting patterns in the symbols targeted for destruction (Table 4.1). Most striking is the fact

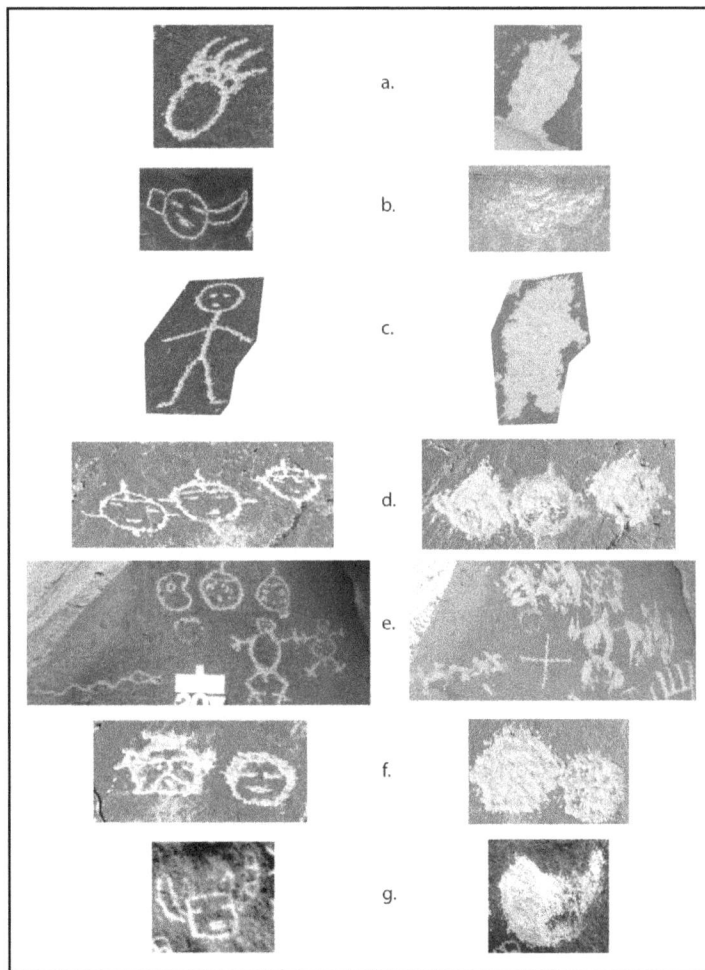

Figure 4.5. Before and after images of obliterated symbols at Tutuveni. a. bear paw, b. One-horn Katsina, c. Máasaw, d. Sun Katsina, e. Máasaw, f. Katsinas, g. Two-horn Katsina.

Table 4.1. Obliterated Symbols.

Symbol	Number Obliterated
Unidentifiable	21
Katsina	12
Sun	12
English Writing	10
Snake	9
Coyote	5
Máasaw	5
Bear/Badger	4
Modern Symbol	4
Corn	3
Qööqöqlö Katsina	3
Cloud	2
Germ God	2
Horn	2
Lizard	2
Parrot	2
Unknown-Bird	2
Unknown	2
Butterfly	1
Extinct-03	1
Mud Head Katsina	1
Rabbit	1
Red Ant	1
Squash	1
Water	1
Total	109

that katsina symbols were targeted more than any other symbol, accounting for 32 percent of the identifiable obliterated symbols. Katsina symbols were targeted far in excess of their actual abundance at Tutuveni, as they account for only seven percent of the intelligible clan symbols present at the site. For example, katsinas were obliterated seven times more often than bear and badger symbols combined, despite the fact that bear/badger symbols are almost twice as common as katsinas across the site. Katsinas have also been targeted for destruction at the Inscription Point Petroglyph site, located approximately 60 km south of Tutuveni (Weaver and Billo 2001:Figure 18).

Although further research is needed, it may be suggested that katsinas have been singled out for destruction more than other symbols because they are a publicly recognized symbol of Hopi religion. In light of the centuries-old conflict between the Hopi and Navajo tribes over ancestral land claims, Tutuveni's existence on what is now Navajo land may threaten Navajo land claims and oral tradition. In this context, erasing overtly Hopi iconography at the site is a way to ensure that archaeological sites match the contemporary political geography.

Two panels provide particularly explicit evidence of the inter-tribal tensions being played out at Tutuveni. Panel 60 Top (Fig. 4.6) contains the scratched words "Damn Hopi Drawing," a reference to the Hopi clan symbols that dominate the site. Panel 137 Southwest (Fig. 4.7) originally contained the words "the Hopi Clans," presumably written by a Hopi tribal member, but a subsequent visitor scratched over this inscription so that it now reads "the ono clans."

Competing signs of a different sort continue to mark land disputes between the Hopi and Navajo tribes. Eight miles from Tutuveni stand the neighboring towns of Tuba City (Navajo) and Munqapi (Hopi), the latter occupying a small island of Hopi territory in the midst of the Navajo reservation. At the boundary between Munqapi and Tuba City (the latter, ironically, was named after an early twentieth-century Hopi village leader who owned fields in the Moenkopi drainage) stands a billboard proclaiming "Hopiland," (Fig. 4.8) despite the fact that the boundary of the bulk of the Hopi reservation is still 30 miles farther to the east. In a parallel contradiction on the Navajo reservation, 40 km north of the Hopi reservation sits Navajo National Monument (Fig. 4.9), where a billboard marking the entrance to the monument reads "Navajo National Monument: Pueblo Indian Ruins." This federally sanctioned statement about identity and cultural patrimony may seem contradictory or reasonable depending on one's perspective.

Figure 4.6. Close-up of Boulder 60 top, with graffiti highlighted; DVD2559.

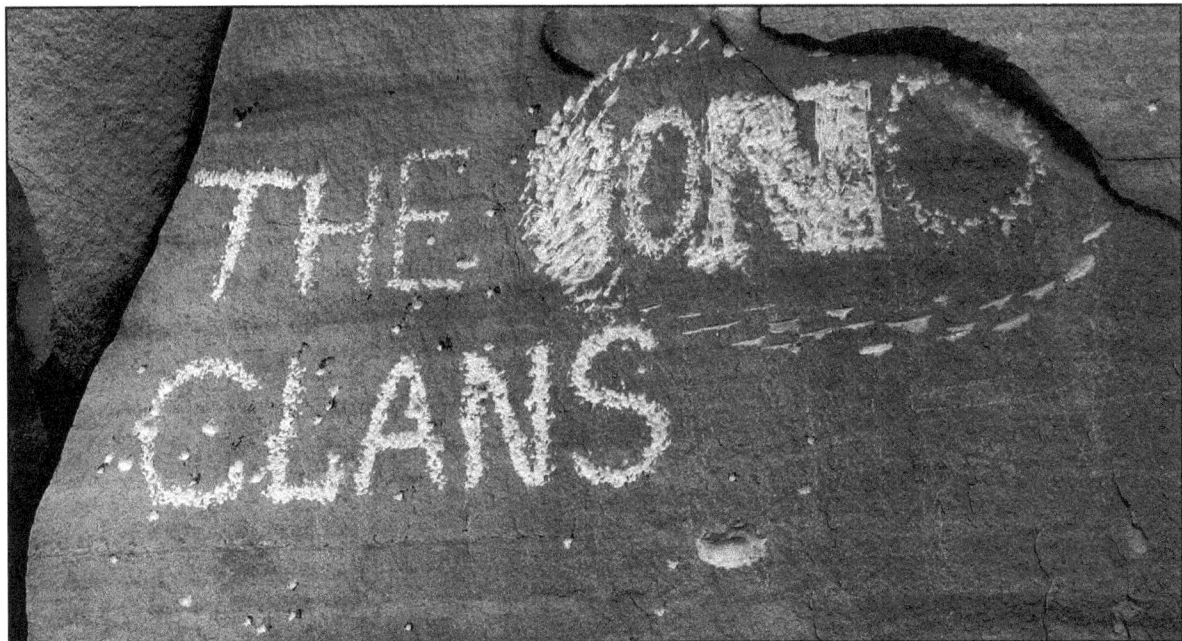

Figure 4.7. Boulder 137 southwest; DVD 1738.

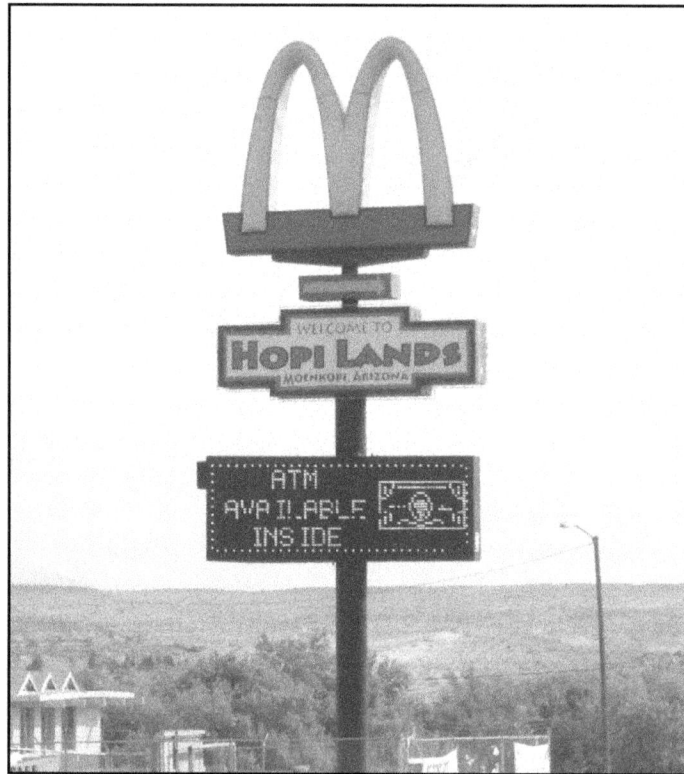

Figure 4.8. Billboard between the towns of Munqapi and Tuba City, Arizona.

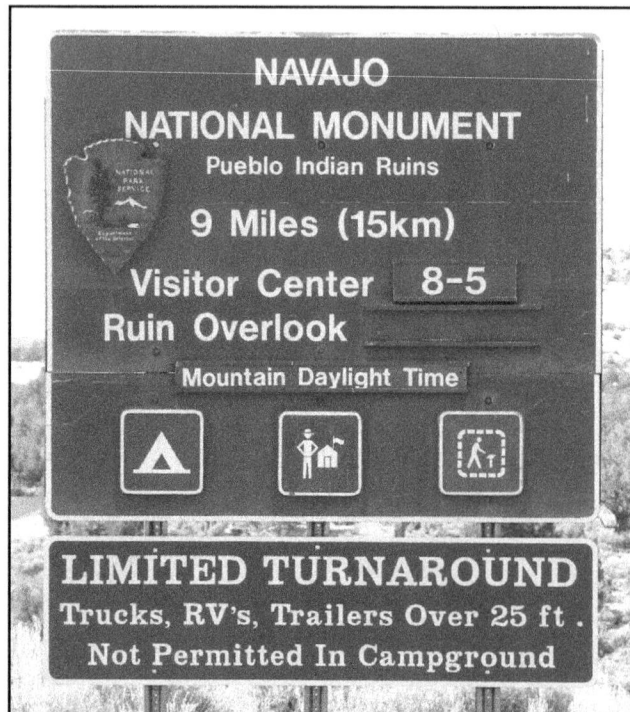

Figure 4.9. Sign at the entrance to the Navajo National Monument, Arizona.

Chapter Five
Tutuveni and Beyond

Although Tutuveni represents the largest and most homogenous concentration of clan symbols known anywhere in the American Southwest, clan petroglyphs are not exclusive to Tutuveni. In fact, the greatest research value of the Tutuveni site is that it facilitates the identification of Hopi clan symbols in places far removed from the modern Hopi reservation. A systematic survey of documented Southwestern rock art for possible clan symbols must await a future study, but a preliminary review has identified a number of symbols mirroring those documented at Tutuveni (Fig. 5.1).

Significantly, each region exhibiting clan symbols typically contains a different subset of the Tutuveni clan symbols. This pattern of highly localized variation in iconic symbols strongly suggests that the symbols reflect small-group identities at each site, rather than reflecting a broader, pan-Southwestern symbolic system (Bernardini 2005a:114–116). This pattern also supports the "gathering of the clans" model of Hopi ethnogenesis that is recorded in Hopi oral tradition, in which clans from across the Southwest converged on the Hopi Mesas to form the Hopi Tribe (Dongoske and others 1997).

It should be emphasized, however, that by itself the presence at an archaeological site of totemic symbols used by contemporary Hopi clans does not necessarily indicate the presence of lineal ancestors in antiquity. In part, this is due to the dynamic nature of clans, both demographically and socially, and the tendency for dispersed clan systems to spread over wide areas to facilitate interaction among different groups.

Caution would also be warranted in drawing such literal links between ancient clan symbols and contemporary Hopi clans because of difficulties in reading ethnicities from the archaeological record (Hutchinson and Smith 1996; Stone 2003; Terrell 2001). From the Hopi perspective, "Hopi" is not an ethnic identity *per se*, but a life philosophy. The migration of Hopi clans was a quest to perfect the practice of *hopivötskwani*, the Hopi path of life (Hill and others 1998:101). Most Hopi clans spent much of their history in a proto-Hopi condition, practicing *hopivötskwani* to the best of their ability, but having not yet found *Tuuwanasavi*, the Earth Center on the Hopi Mesas, where their spiritual compact with *Máasaw* would be fulfilled. The interpretation of signs of Hopi practice outside the Hopi Mesas is therefore complex, even, or especially, from a Hopi perspective (Bernardini 2008).

Reading ethnic identity from material culture, even unusually iconographic material like totemic petroglyphs, is clearly a delicate undertaking. The identification of regions displaying petroglyphs similar to clan symbols found at Tutuveni should be taken as a starting point for research on ethnicity and identity, not a conclusion regarding the presence of Hopi clans in a simplistic fashion.

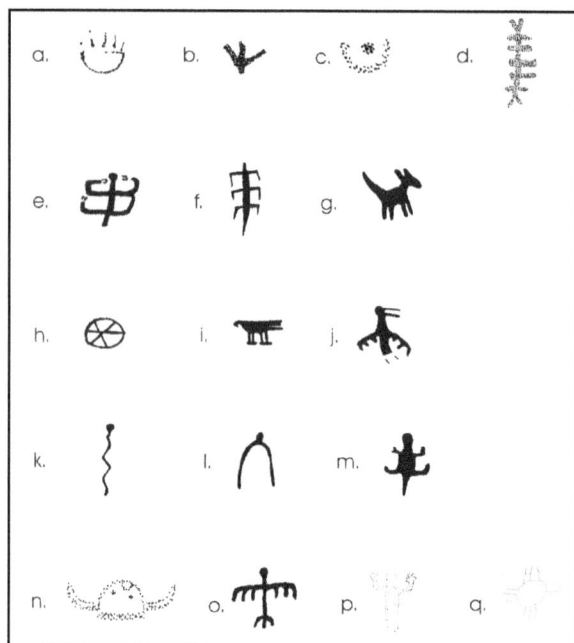

Figure 5.1. Examples of possible clan symbols outside the Hopi Mesas: a-d. Puerco Ruin (after Bock 1988), e. Chavez Pass SE (Bernardini 2002), f. Chavez Pass SW (Bernardini 2002), g. Pollock Ruin (Bernardini 2002), h-j. Homol'ovi II (after Cole 1987), k-l. Homol'ovi IV (after Cole 1987), m. Cottonwood Pueblo (after Cole 1987), n. Glen Canyon (redrawn after Turner 1963), o. Rattlesnake Pueblo (redrawn after Duff and Kintigh 1995), p. 42GA3938 in Capitol Reef National Park, Utah (Bernardini 2007), q. 42GA1876, southern Utah (Bernardini 2007).

PETRIFIED FOREST

The Petrified Forest National Park is located about 200 km east of Flagstaff, Arizona. Within its boundaries is Puerco Ruin, a large pueblo of more than 100 rooms dating from approximately A.D. 1250–1350 (Burton 1990). Most of the petroglyphs resembling Tutuveni clan symbols within the park boundaries are found in close association with this site. The Hopi Tribe considers Puerco Ruin to be an ancestral Hopi site, and the presence of more than 700 sherds of Hopi-made Jeddito Yellow Ware vessels at the site suggests that residents of Puerco Ruin had direct contact with residents of Hopi

villages (Vint and Burton 1990).

The Puerco Ruin petroglyphs, consisting of more than 800 images on 101 boulders, are reported in Burton (1990) and Bock (1988). Examination of the Puerco Ruin petroglyphs resulted in the identification of 80 elements that closely resembled symbols at the Tutuveni Petroglpyh Site (Bernardini 2005a:Table 4.3). Bear/badger, bird, butterfly, coyote, eagle, greasewood, katsina, lizard, horn, parrot, and snake symbols were present, but bear and bird symbols were unusually common (Fig. 5.1). In addition, a recurring mountain lion symbol was observed alongside these established clan symbols. The mountain lion symbol is not found at Tutuveni; therefore, it may have been a totem of an extinct clan local to Puerco Ruin. Patricia McCreery also observed possible moon and sun symbols at the Boundary site and Newspaper Rock petroglyph clusters, located some distance from Puerco Ruin. The Petrified Forest also contains evidence of continued historical visitation and clan-symbol signing very similar to images at Tutuveni, suggesting continuity of practice over time at both locations (Fig. 5.2).

ANDERSON MESA

Anderson Mesa, a basalt plateau extending more than 65 km southeast from Flagstaff, Arizona, was the center of a northern Sinagua occupation from about A.D. 1275–1400 (Bernardini and Brown 2004). Six large pueblos were occupied during this period, all of which are considered by the Hopi Tribe to be ancestral villages. The largest site is known as Chavez Pass, or *Nuvakwewtaqa*, a Hopi word meaning "a butte with snow belt on." At least 10 different Hopi clans trace their migrations through Anderson Mesa villages, including the Eagle, Hawk, Moon, Lizard, Rabbit, Sand, Tobacco and Water clans (Courlander 1971:72–73;

a.

b.

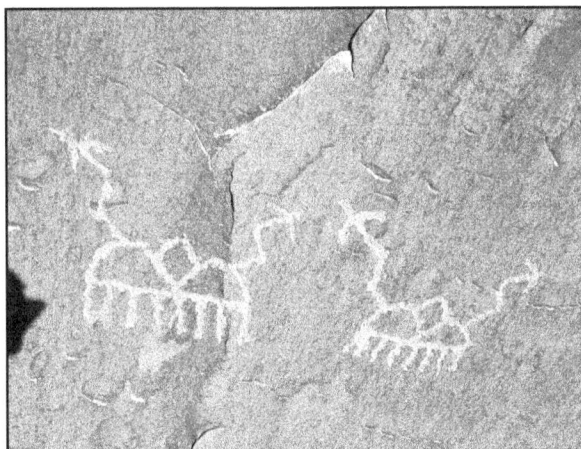

c.

Figure 5.2. Examples of historical revisitation of ancestral Hopi places: a) Petrified Forest (photograph by Patricia McCreery); b) Tutuveni (photograph by Wesley Bernardini); c) Tutuveni (photograph by Wesley Bernardini).

Fewkes 1900:597). The decorated ceramic assemblages of the four Anderson Mesa sites with substantial post-A.D. 1300 occupations (Chavez Pass SW, Chavez Pass SE, Kinni-kinick, and Grapevine) contain between 18 and 73 percent Jeddito Yellow Ware ceramics, indicating frequent contact with Hopi Mesa villages.

Chavez Pass SW, Chavez Pass SE, Pollock, and Kinnikinick are closely associated with petroglyph panels containing a total of almost 400 images. Survey and analysis of these petroglyphs (Bernardini 2005a:100–116) identified 139 images that closely resembled Tutuveni clan symbols, including bear/badger, butterfly, corn, coyote, katsina, lizard, horn, and snake, but butterfly, corn, coyote, horn and lizard symbols were unusually common (Fig. 5.1). An additional recurring symbol, dubbed rabbit ears for its resemblance to television antennae, may be a symbol of a local extinct clan. The pattern of local variability in totemic symbols is especially pronounced at Anderson Mesa sites. Chavez Pass SW and Chavez Pass SE, for example, are located a mere 125 m apart and were both occupied from about A.D. 1275–1375, yet they contain non-overlapping sets of recurring images, including butterfly and rabbit ears at Chavez Pass SW and corn and horn at Chavez SE.

HOMOL'OVI

The Homol'ovi region is located 80 km south of the Hopi Mesas, along the Middle Little Colorado River, where seven large villages were occupied between approximately A.D. 1260–1400 (Adams 2004). At least 10 Hopi clans, including the Corn, Water, Tobacco, Rabbit, Coyote, Eagle, Sun, Sun Forehead, Sand, and Reed clans, trace their migration through the Homol'ovi pueblos (Courlander 1971, 1982; Fewkes 1900). The post-A.D. 1350 ceramic assemblages of Homol'ovi villages are dominated by Jeddito Yellow Ware vessels, with an estimated 100,000 vessels in all, which were transported by hand from Hopi villages (Adams 2002). Many Hopi consultants, and some archaeologists, consider the later Homol'ovi villages, especially Homol'ovi II, to have been Hopi villages that were ethnically, politically, and ritually comparable to Awat'ovi or Orayvi at the same time period (Adams 2002).

Petroglyphs at Homol'ovi II, Homol'ovi IV, and Cottonwood have been reported by Cole (1987, 1992). Out of a total of 1,110 images closely associated with these three sites, 236 were identified as potential clan symbols based on similarities to Tutuveni images, including bear/badger, butterfly, corn, coyote, katsina, lizard, oak, horn, snake, and squash; however, katsina and snake symbols were unusually common (Bernardini 2005a). Several recurring images not found at Tutuveni may be symbols of local, extinct clans, including coatis, mountain lions, rabbit ears, and scorpions.

ZUNI

The Zuni region, located approximately 150 km southeast of the Hopi Mesas, was the closest puebloan neighbor to Hopi after the population movements of the late A.D. 1200s and A.D. 1300s, and contained populations that were more closely culturally related to Hopi than any others in the Southwest (Ladd 1979; Woodbury 1979). The migration traditions of several Hopi clans mention ancestral villages in the Zuni region (Fewkes 1900). Some sites on the Hopi Mesas are said to have been occupied by clans who came from, and in some cases returned to, Zuni.

Petroglyph images from one Zuni village, Rattlesnake Point, contain 24 potential clan symbols including bird, butterfly, coyote, katsina, lizard, and snake (Duff and Kintigh 1995).

Bird and mountain lion symbols are unusually common (Bernardini 2005a:Table 4.3). Recurring images that may be local, extinct clans, include scorpions and mountain lions.

UTAH

Some of the earliest identifications of potential Hopi clan symbols outside the Hopi region were made during the Glen Canyon Project (Turner 1963). Turner (1963:6) identified Style 2 rock art as "linked with Hopi revisitation of the canyons from the fourteenth century to the present" based on the common association of Jeddito Yellow Ware pottery with the petroglyphs, and similarities to the "Moenave petroglyphs," a reference to Tutuveni. Possible clan symbols recorded in Glen Canyon include bear/badger, flute, horn, katsina, and water. The presence of Style 2 elements across southern Utah (Bernardini 2007) supports the migration traditions of Hopi clans such as the Badger, Fire, Flute, Greasewood, Snake, Horn, Spider, Reed, Antelope, Sand, Bearstrap, and Katsina clans, which recount movement through areas far to the north of the Hopi Mesas (Curtis 1922:78–79; Ferguson 1998; Fewkes 1894:106).

CONSIDERATIONS IN REGIONAL COMPARISONS

Any given population may have produced petroglyphs in a number of different contexts for different reasons, and possibly even in the same context for different reasons. To restrict analysis to petroglpyh elements that are most likely to pertain to group identity, it is recommended to follow the protocol established by Bernardini (2005a:99–100). Briefly, analysis should focus on petroglyphs that:

1) are located in close spatial proximity to a known, residential village, excluding special purpose activity areas, though exceptions, most obviously pilgrimage sites like Tutuveni, may apply. 2) exhibit the style expected for Pueblo IV (post-A.D. 1300) rock art in the study area (McCreery and Malotki 1994; Pilles 1975; Schaafsma 1980; Turner 1963), the time period after which totemic symbols appear most frequently. 3) share morphological characteristics of known totemic symbols, namely isolation (for example, not part of a narrative picture), standardization (such as, a spare, conventionalized style, like a company logo), theme (primarily restricted to plants, animals, meteorological phenomena, and cultural objects), and repetition (for example, the symbol should be found multiple times, ideally, at least three times in association with a given village).

Restricting analysis in this manner will not only help to identify symbols of known clans, but can also highlight potential symbols of extinct clans.

FUTURE RESEARCH

The analyses of the Tutuveni petroglyphs presented here only scratch the surface of the site's potential. With the detailed locational information available for every element, spatial analysis of symbol distribution and covariation could reveal much about the social, political, and ritual relationships of the groups who visited the site. Relative amounts of repatination could be used to more finely order the sequence of symbols at the site, opening up exciting avenues for diachronic study of clan dynamics. The historical photographs included on the DVD could be used to trace the evolution of panels over the past 80 years. Comparisons of symbol frequency and spatial relationships with historical records and censuses could shed further light the dynamics of twentieth-century Hopi clan identity and interrelationships. Further consultation with Hopi advisors could shed light on non-clan symbols at Tutuveni, and recover additional traditional knowledge about extinct clans or relationships between clans.

CONCLUSION

Tutuveni is a unique site, a potential Rosetta Stone of Hopi clan iconography in the American Southwest. Regrettably, the site has been heavily damaged by vandals who carved deep scars in the records left by generations of Hopi clans. By comparing modern and historical photographs it has been possible to reconstruct much of the site's original condition, establishing this report as the definitive resource for the site. It is hoped that this resource will facilitate the identification and interpretation of Hopi clan iconography across the Southwestern region.

This project was the result of a collaborative effort between academic archaeologists and the Hopi and Navajo tribes. The common interest shared by all three groups was a desire to document an important cultural resource before it was further damaged, and to collect information to make a case for protecting it. This type of preservation research is a productive model for academic archaeology, striking a balance between pure research and salvage work. This project also illustrates the mutual benefits of archaeology conducted as a collaborative enterprise among archaeologists and descendant communities.

References Cited

Aberle, David F.
    1970 Comments. In *Reconstructing Prehistoric Pueblo Societies*, edited by William A. Longacre, pp. 215–223. University of New Mexico Press, Albuquerque.

Adams, E. Charles
    1991 *The Origin and Development of the Pueblo Katsina Cult*. University of Arizona Press, Tucson.

    2002 *Homol'ovi: An Ancient Hopi Settlement Cluster in Northeastern Arizona*. University of Arizona Press, Tucson.

    2004 Homol'ovi: A 13th–14th Century Settlement Cluster in Northeastern Arizona. In *The Protohistoric Pueblo World, A.D. 1275–1600*, edited by E. Charles Adams and Andrew I. Duff, pp. 119–127. University of Arizona Press, Tucson.

Balsom, James
    1993 Native Americans of the Grand Canyon. In *Hiking the Grand Canyon*, by John Annerino, pp.6–13. Sierra Club Books, San Francisco.

Bernardini, Wesley
    2005a *Hopi Oral Tradition and the Archeology of Identity*. The University of Arizona Press, Tucson.

    2005b Reconsidering Spatial and Temporal Aspects of Prehistoric Cultural Identity: A Case Study from the American Southwest. *American Antiquity* 70(1):31–54.

    2007 *Ethnographic Overview for the Grand Staircase-Escalante National Monument*. Hopi Cultural Preservation Office, Kykotsmovi, Arizona.

    2008 Identity as History: Hopi Clans and the Curation of Oral Tradition. Journal of Anthropological Research Vol 64(4):483-509.

Bernardini, Wesley, and Gary M. Brown
    2004 The Formation of Settlement Clusters on Anderson Mesa. In *The Protohistoric Pueblo World, A.D. 1275–1600*, edited by E. Charles Adams, and Andrew I. Duff, pp. 108–118. University of Arizona Press, Tucson.

Bock, Frank
    1988 *Petrified Forest National Park Rock Art Survey Preliminary Report*. Report submitted to the Western Archaeological and Conservation Center, National Park Service, U.S. Department of the Interior, Tucson, Arizona.

Bradfield, Richard M.
    1973 *A Natural History of Associations: A Study in the Meaning of Community* Vol. 2. International Universities Press, New York.

Brugge, David
    1994 *The Navajo-Hopi Land Dispute: An American Tragedy*. University of New Mexico Press, Albuquerque.

Burton, Jeffery F. (editor)
  1990 *Archaeological Investigations at Puerco Ruin, Petrified Forest National Park.* Publications in Anthropology 54. Western Archaeological and Conservation Center, National Park Service, Tucson.

Cheremisin, David
  2002 Renovation of Ancient Compositions by Modern Indigenous Visitors in Altai, Southern Siberia: Vandalism or Creation? *Rock Art Research* 19(2):105–108.

Cole, Sally J.
  1987 Notes and Photographs from the Homol'ovi Rock Art Recording Project, directed by Sally Cole. Manuscript on file Homol'ovi Research Program, Arizona State Museum, Tucson.

  1992 *Katsina Iconography in Homol'ovi Rock Art, Central Little Colorado River Valley, Arizona.* The Arizona Archaeologist No. 25. Arizona Archaeological Society, Tucson.

Colton, Harold S.
  1946 Fools Names like Fools Faces. *Plateau* 19(1):1–8.

  1959 *Hopi Katsina Dolls.* University of New Mexico Press, Albuquerque.

  1960 *Black Sand.* University of New Mexico Press, Albuquerque.

Colton, Mary, and Harold S. Colton
  1931 Petroglyphs, the Record of a Great Adventure. *American Anthropologist* 33:32–35.

Colwell-Chanthaphonh, Chip, and T. J. Ferguson (editors)
  2006 *Collaboration in Archaeological Practice: Engaging Descendent Communities.* Alta Mira Press, Walnut Creek, California.

Connelly, John C.
  1979 Hopi Social Organization. In *Southwest*, edited by Alfonso Ortiz, pp. 539–543. Handbook of North American Indians, Volume 9, William C. Sturtevant, general editor, Smithsonian Institution, Washington, D.C.

Courlander, Harold
  1971 *The Fourth World of the Hopis: The Epic Story of the Hopi Indians as Preserved in Their Legends and Traditions.* University of New Mexico Press, Albuquerque.

  1982 *Hopi Voices: Recollections, Traditions, and Narratives of the Hopi Indians.* University of New Mexico Press, Albuquerque.

Curtis, Russell S.
  1922 *The North American Indian*, Vol. 12. The Plimpton Press, Norwood.

Dongoske, Kurt, Michael Yeatts, Rosa Anyon, and T. J. Ferguson
  1997 Archaeological Cultures and Cultural Affiliation: Hopi and Zuni Perspectives in the American Southwest. *American Antiquity* 62(2):600–608.

Duff, Andrew I., and Keith W. Kintigh
  1995 *Lyman Lake Rock Art Site.* National Register of Historic Places Registration Form, Manuscript on file at the United States Department of the Interior, National Park Service.

Eggan, Fred
  1950 *Social Organization of the Western Pueblos.* University of Chicago, Chicago.

Eggan, Fred (cont'd)
1994 The Hopi Indians: With Special Reference to Their Cosmology or World-View. In *Kachinas in the Pueblo World*, edited by Polly Schaafsma, pp. 7–16. University of New Mexico Press, Albuquerque.

Eiseman, Fred
1959 The Hopi Salt Trail. *Plateau* 32(2):25–32.

Ferguson, T. J.
1998 *Öngtupqa niqw Pisisvayu (Salt Canyon and the Colorado River): The Hopi People and the Grand Canyon*. Report on file at the Hopi Cultural Preservation Office, Kykotsmovi, Arizona.

Ferguson, T. J., and Micah Lomaomvaya
1999 *Hoopoq'auqam niqw Wukoskyavi (Those Who Went to the Northeast and Tonto Basin): Hopi-Salado Cultural Affiliation Study*. Report on file at the Hopi Cultural Preservation Office, Kykotsmovi, Arizona.

Fewkes, Jesse W.
1892 A Few Tusayan Pictographs. *American Anthropologist* 5:9–26.

1894 The Snake Ceremonials at Walpi. *A Journal of American Ethnology and Archaeology* 4:105–124.

1897 Tusayan Totemic Signatures. *American Anthropologist* 19(1):1–11.

1900 Tusayan Migration Traditions. In *19th Annual Report of the Bureau of American Ethnology for the Years 1897–1898,* Pt. 2, pp. 573–634. Government Printing Office, Washington, D.C.

Frigout, Arlette
1979 Hopi Ceremonial Organization. In *Southwest*, edited by Alfonso Ortiz, pp. 564–76. Handbook of North American Indians, Volume 9, William C. Sturtevant, general editor, Smithsonian Institution, Washington, D.C.

Gaines, Sylvia and Warren M. Gaines
1997 Simulating Success or Failure: Another Look at Small-Population Dynamics. *American Antiquity* 62(4):683–697.

Hammond, George P., and Agapito Rey (editors)
1929 *Expedition into New Mexico made by Antonio de Espejo, 1582–1583; as Revealed by the Journal of Diego Perez de Luxan*. Quivira Society Publication No. 1. Quivira Society, Los Angeles.

Harvey, Fred
1970 *The Watchtower Guide*. Published by the author, An Amfac Resort, Grand Canyon National Park, Arizona.

Hedges, Ken
1990 Repainting in Kumeyaay Rock Art: Vandalism, Defacement, or Renewal? *American Indian Rock Art* 16:63–70.

Hill, Kenneth, Emory Sekaquaptewa, Mary E. Black, Ekkehart Malotki, and Michael Lomatuway'ma (editors)
1998 *Hopi Dictionary, Hopiikwa Lavaytutuveni: A Hopi-English Dictionary of the Third Mesa Dialect*. University of Arizona Press, Tucson.

Hooper, Mildred, and C. Hooper
1968 Shrine on the Hopi Salt Trail. *Arizona Days Magazine*, April, pp. 46–48.

1977 Shrine of the Clan Rocks. *Outdoor Arizona*, June, pp. 20–23.

Hutchinson, John and Anthony D. Smith (editors)
  1996 *Ethnicity*. Oxford University Press, Oxford.

Kintigh, Keith W. and Albert Ammerman
  1982 Heuristic Approaches to Spatial Analysis in Archaeology. *American Antiquity* 47(1):31–63.

Ladd, Edmund
  1979 Zuni Social and Political Organization. In *Southwest*, edited by Alfonso Ortiz, pp. 482–491.
    Handbook of North American Indians, Volume 9, William C. Sturtevant, general editor, Smithsonian
    Institution, Washington, D.C.

Levy, Jerrold
  1992 *Orayvi Revisited: Social Stratification in an 'Egalitarian' Society*. School of American Research
    Press, Santa Fe.

Lowie, Robert H.
  1929 *Notes on Hopi Clans*. Anthropological Papers of the American Museum of Natural History, Vol. 30,
    pp. 363–388. American Museum of Natural History, New York.

Lyons, Patrick
  2003 *Ancestral Hopi Migrations*. Anthropological Papers of the University of Arizona Number 68.
    University of Arizona Press, Tucson.

Mallery, Garrick
  1886 Pictographs of the North American Indians: A Preliminary Paper. In *4th Annual Report of the Bureau
    of American Ethnology, 1882–1883*, pp. 3–256. Smithsonian Institution, Washington, D.C.

McCreery, Patricia, and Ekkehart Malotki
  1994 *Tapamveni: The Rock Art Galleries of Petrified Forest and Beyond*. Petrified Forest Museum
    Association, Petrified Forest, Arizona.

McNitt, Frank
  1964 *Navaho Expedition: A Journal of a Military Reconnaissance from Santa Fe, New Mexico to the
    Navajo Country Made in 1849, by Lieutenant James H. Simpson*. University of Oklahoma Press,
    Norman.

Michaelis, Helen
  1981 Willowsprings: A Hopi Petroglyph Site. *Journal of New World Archaeology* 4(2):2–23.

Mindeleff, Cosmos
  1891 Traditional History of Tusayan. In *8th Annual Report of the Bureau of American Ethnology for the
    Years 1886–1887*, pp. 16–41. Government Printing Office, Washington, D.C.

Morphy, Howard
  1989 Introduction. In *Animals into Art*, edited by Howard Morphy, pp. 1–17. Unwin Hyman, London.

Murdock, George P.
  1949 *Social Structure*. The Macmillan Company, New York.

Parsons, Elsie C.
  1923 The Hopi Wöwöchim Ceremony in 1920. *American Anthropologist* 25:156–187.

  1925 *A Pueblo Indian Journal, 1920–1921*. Memoirs of the American Anthropological Association 32.
    American Anthropological Association, Menasha, Wisconsin.

Parsons, Elsie (cont'd)
    1933 *Hopi and Zuni Ceremonialism*. Memoirs of the American Anthropological Association 39. American Anthropological Association, Meanasha, Wisconsin.

    1936 The House-Clan Complex of the Pueblos. In *Essays in Anthropology Presented to A. L. Kroeber,* edited by Robert H. Lowie, pp. 239–231. University of California Press, Berkeley.

Parsons, Elsie C. (editor)
    1969 *Hopi Journal of Alexander M. Stephen*. Columbia University Press, New York.

Pilles, Peter
    1975 Petroglyphs of the Little Colorado River Valley, Arizona. In *American Indian Rock Art: Papers Presented at the 1974 Rock Art Symposium,* edited by S. T. Grove. San Juan County Museum Association, Farmington, New Mexico.

Plog, Stephen, and Julie Solometo
    1997 The Never-Changing and the Ever-Changing: The Evolution of Western Pueblo Ritual. *Cambridge Archaeological Journal* 7(2):161–182.

Schaafsma, Polly
    1980 *Indian Rock Art of the Southwest*. University of New Mexico Press, Albuquerque.

Schlegel, Alice
    1992 African Political Models in the American Southwest: Hopi as an Internal Frontier Society. *American Anthropologist* 94(2):376–397.

Shennan, Stephen
    1997 *Quantifying Archaeology*. Edinburgh University Press, Edinburgh, Scottland.

Simmons, Leo
    1942 *Sun Chief: The Autobiography of a Hopi Indian*. Yale University Press, New Haven.

Steward, Julian
    1937 Ecological Aspects of Southwestern Society. *Anthropos* 32:87–104.

Stone, Tammy
    2003 Social Identity and Ethnic Interaction in the Western Pueblos of the American Southwest. *Journal of Archaeological Method and Theory* 10(1):31–67.

Swidler, Nina, Kurt E. Dongoske, Roger Anyon, and Alan S. Downer (editors)
    1997 *Native Americans and Archaeologists: Stepping Stones to Common Ground*. AltaMira Press, Walnut Creek, Califonia.

Tessman, Norm
    1986 National Register of Historic Places Inventory Nomination Form for the Tutuveni Petroglyph Site. Manuscript on file at the United States Department of the Interior.

Terrell, John Edward
    2001 Introduction. In *Archaeology, Language, and History: Essays on Culture and Ethnicity*, edited by John E. Terrell, pp. 1–10. Bergin and Garvey, Westport, Connecticut.

Titiev, Mischa
    1937 A Hopi Salt Expedition. *American Anthropologist* 39:244–258.

Titiev, Mischa (cont'd)
    1944 *Old Oraibi: A Study of the Hopi Indians of Third Mesa.* Papers of the Peabody Museum of American Archaeology and Ethnology 22(1). Harvard Museum, Cambridge.

Turner, Christy
    1963 *Petroglyphs of the Glen Canyon Region.* Bulletin No. 38, Glen Canyon Series No. 4. Northern Arizona Society of Science and Art, Flagstaff, Arizona.

Vint, James, and Jeffery Burton
    1990 Ceramics. In *Archaeological Investigations at Puerco Ruin, Petrified Forest National Park,* edited by Jeffery Burton, pp. 97–126. Publications in Anthropology 54. Western Archaeological and Conservation Center, National Park Service, Tucson.

Waters, Frank
    1963 *Book of the Hopi.* Penguin Books, New York.

Weaver, Donald
    1984 Images on Stone: The Prehistoric Rock Art of the Colorado Plateau. *Plateau* 55:1–32.

Weaver, Donald, R. Mark, and Evelyn Billo
    2001 Inscription Point: Too Little Too Late? *American Indian Rock Art* 27:137–150.

Whiteley, Peter
    1985 Unpacking Hopi 'Clans': Another Vintage Model Out of Africa? *Journal of Anthropological Research* 41(4):359–374.

    1986 Unpacking Hopi 'Clans' II: Further Questions about Hopi Descent Groups. *Journal of Anthropological Research* 42(1):69–79.

    1988 *Deliberate Acts: Changing Hopi Culture Through the Oraibi Split.* University of Arizona Press, Tucson.

    2003 Leslie White's Hopi Ethnography: Of Practice and In Theory. *Journal of Anthropological Research* 59:151–181.

Woodbury, Richard
    1979 Zuni Prehistory and History to 1850. In *Southwest,* edited by Alfonso Ortiz, pp. 467–473. Handbook of North American Indians, Volume 9, Willian C. Sturtevant, general editor, Smithsonian Institution, Washington, D.C.

Young, Jane
    1988 *Signs from the Ancestors: Zuni Cultural Symbolism and Perceptions of Rock Art.* University of New Mexico Press, Albuquerque.

Appendix I
Additional Images

a.

b.

Figure I.1. Example of vandalism: Boulder 17 South in a. 1930 (photo Harold Colton, copyright Museum of Northern Arizona; DVD1815) and b. 2004 (photo Wesley Bernardini; DVD0384); see also DVD0370-0388, 1812-1815, 1856-1857, 1903-1904, 1983, 2029-2030, 2096, 2109-2110, 2133-2134, and 2296-2302.

a.

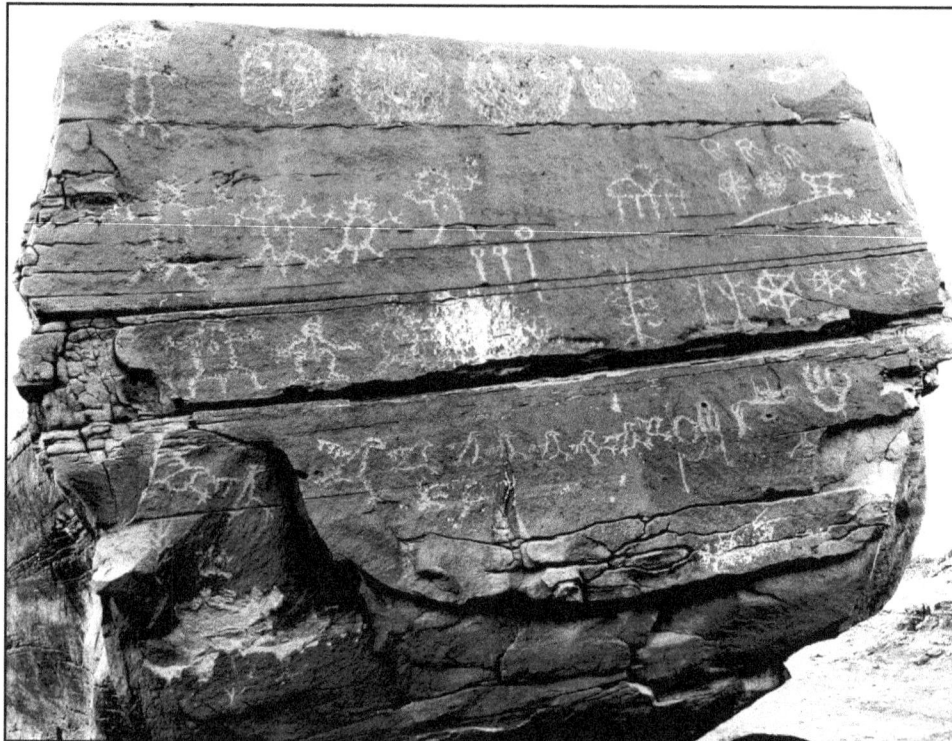

b.

Figure I.2. Example of vandalism: Boulder 17 Southeast in a. 1930 (photo Harold Colton, copyright Museum of Northern Arizona; DVD1816) and b. 2004 (photo Wesley Bernardini; DVD0391); see also DVD0389-0409, 2031-2033, 2303-2309, and 2484.

a.

b.

Figure I.3. Example of vandalism: Boulder 18 North in a. 1930 (photo Harold Colton, copyright Museum of Northern Arizona; DVD1817) and b. 2004 (photo Wesley Bernardini; DVD0429); see also DVD0426-0444, 1817, 2136, and 2310-2311.

a.

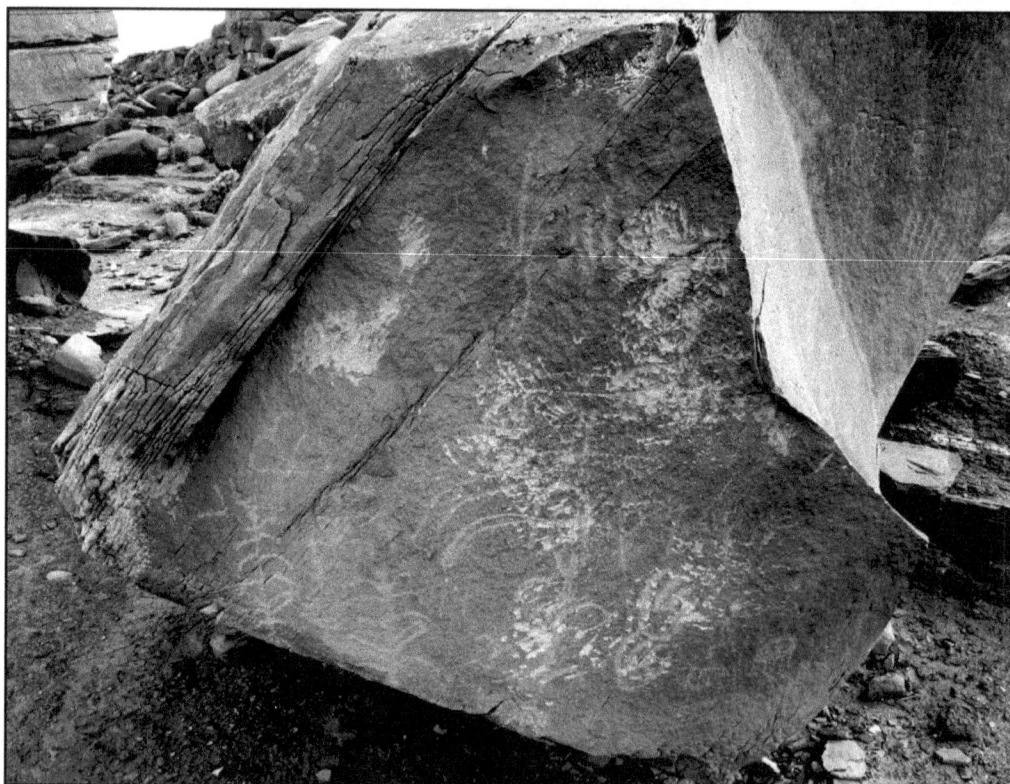

b.

Figure I.4. Example of vandalism: Boulder 18 Southwest in a. 1930 (photo Harold Colton, copyright Museum of Northern Arizona; DVD1819) and b. 2004 (photo Wesley Bernardini; DVD0470); see also DVD0468-0480, 1819, 2319, and 2320.

a.

b.

Figure I.5. Example of vandalism: Boulder 30 South in a. 1978 (photo Helen Michaelis, copyright UCLA Rock Art Archive; DVD1862) and b. 2004 (photo Wesley Bernardini; DVD0558); see also DVD0554-0579, 1824-1828, 1911-1914, 1987, 2040-2043, 2091, 2114, 2140-2142, 2337-2354, 2485-2488, and 2557-2558.

a.

b.

Figure I.6. Example of vandalism: Boulder 36 East in a. 1930 (photo Harold Colton, copyright Museum of Northern Arizona; DVD1831) and b. 2004 (photo Wesley Bernardini; DVD0746); see also DVD0745-0746, 1831, 1869, 1921, and 2371-2373.

a.

b.

Figure I.7. Example of vandalism: Boulder 37 Top in a. 1930 (photo Harold Colton, copyright Museum of Northern Arizona; DVD1832) and b. 2004 (photo Wesley Bernardini; DVD0750); see also DVD0749-0767, 1832, 1870, 1922-1923, 1991, 2097, 2148, 2374-2380, and 2499.

a.

b.

Figure I.8. Example of vandalism: Boulder 43 South in a. 1930 (photo Harold Colton, copyright Museum of Northern Arizona; DVD1834) and b. 2004 (photo Wesley Bernardini; DVD0811); see also DVD0808-0822, 1834, 1873, 1994, 2051, 2098, 2149-2151, 2384-2389, and 2500-2502.

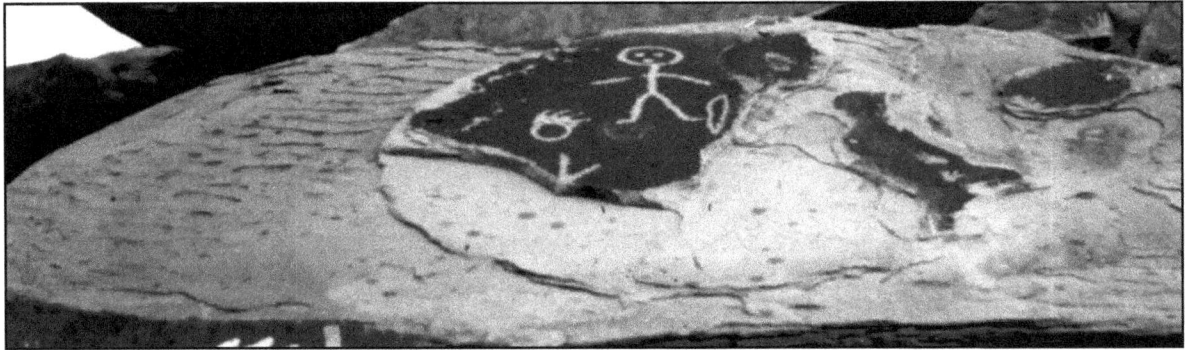

a.

b.

Figure I.9. Example of vandalism: Boulder 45 Top in a. 1978 (photo Helen Michaelis, copyright UCLA Rock Art Archive; DVD1874) and b. 2004 (photo Wesley Bernardini; DVD0840); DVD0837-0849, 1874, 1995, 2052, 2390, and 2503-2505.

a.

b.

Figure I.10. Example of vandalism: Boulder 48 Northeast, lower left quarter, in a. 1930 (photo Harold Colton, copyright Museum of Northern Arizona; DVD1836) and b. 2004 (photo Wesley Bernardini; DVD0867); see also DVD0866-0867, 0871-0874, 0877, 0913, 0917, 0922-0923, 0929-0930, 1836, 1925, and 2509.

a.

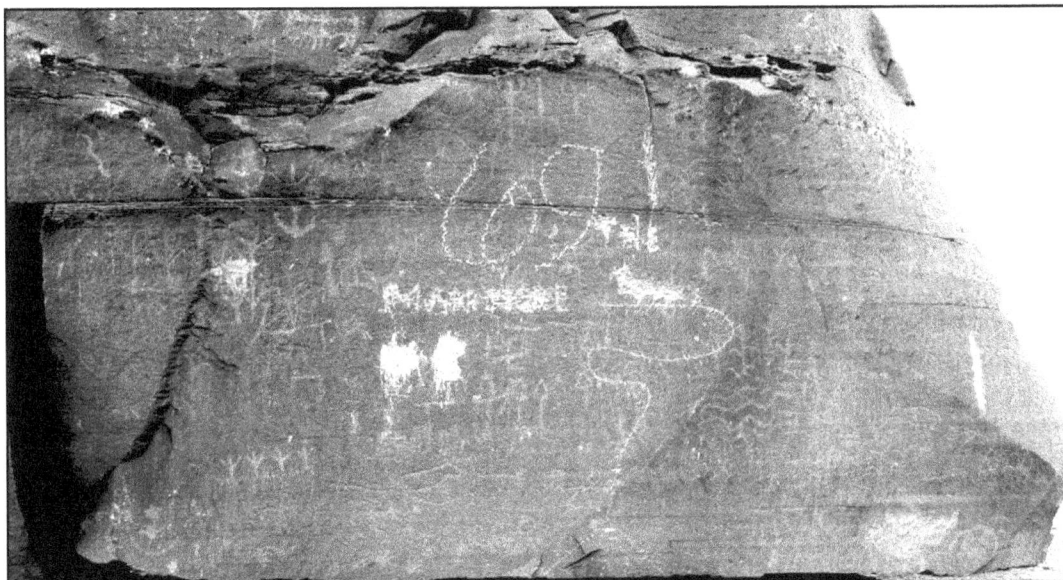

b.

Figure I.11. Example of vandalism: Boulder 48 Northeast, lower right quarter, in a. 1930 (photo Harold Colton, copyright Museum of Northern Arizona; DVD1835) and b. 2004 (photo Wesley Bernardini; DVD0869); see also DVD0868, 0876, 0915, 0919, and 1835.

a.

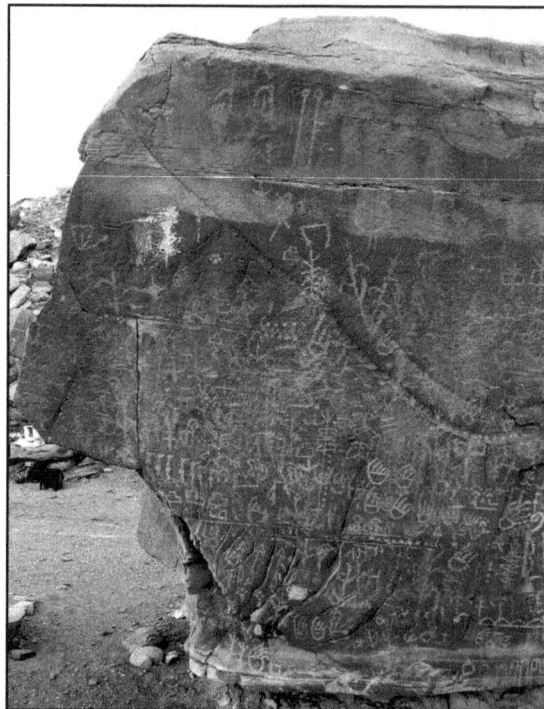

b.

Figure I.12. Example of vandalism: Boulder 48 Southwest, left third, in a. 1930 (photo Harold Colton, copyright Museum of Northern Arizona; DVD1842) and b. 2004 (photo Wesley Bernardini; DVD1021); see also DVD1020-1021, 1025-1026, 1028, 1030-1031, 1075-1080, 1091-1094, 1098, 1842, 1882, 1943-1946, 1952, 1955, 2067, 069, 2074, 2402, 2415, 2525-2526, and 2561-2562.

a.

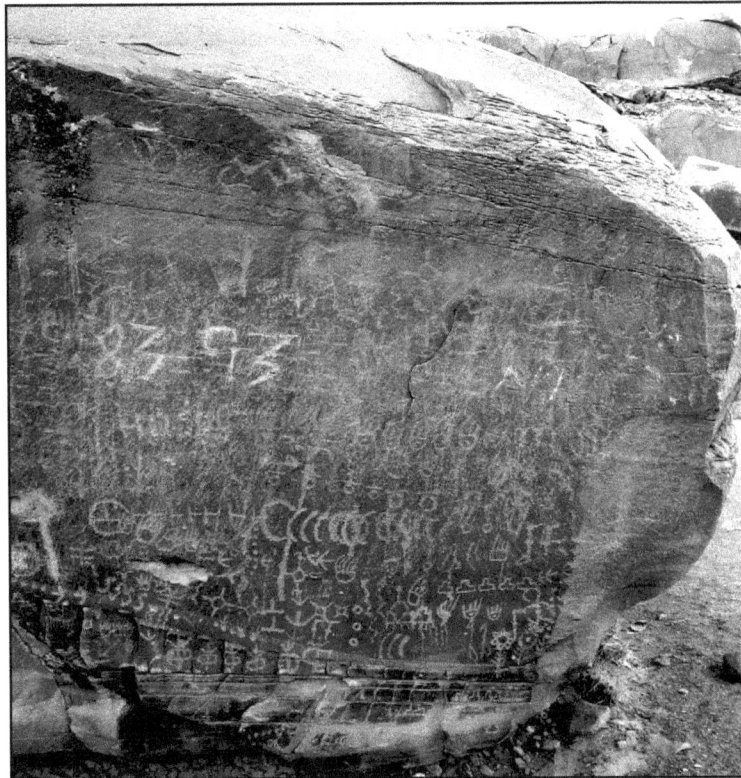

b.

Figure I.13. Example of vandalism: Boulder 48 Southwest, right third, in a. 1930 (photo Harold Colton, copyright Museum of Northern Arizona; DVD1841) and b. 2004 (photo Wesley Bernardini; DVD1024); see also DVD1023-1024, 1029, 1032, 1055-1064, 1066-1071, 1073, 1084-1088, 1095-1097, 1099-1101, 1841, 1880-1881, 1948-1949, 1951, 1954, 2072, 2161, 2403, 2416, and 2527-2528.

a.

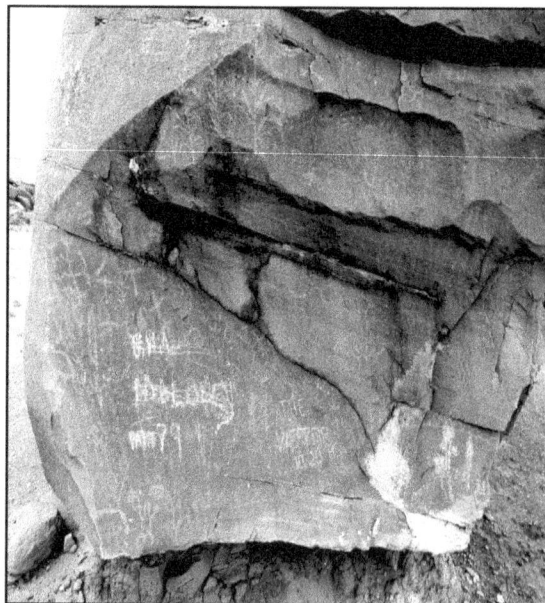

b.

Figure I.14. Example of vandalism: Boulder 48 Northwest, bottom half, in a. 1978 (photo Helen Michaelis, copright UCLA Rock Art Archive; DVD1876) and b. 2004 (photo Wesley Bernardini; DVD0943); see also DVD0940-0943, 0945-1949, 0951-1952, 1954-0956, 0958, 0970-0972, 1876, and 2153-2154.

a.

b.

Figure I.15. Example of vandalism: Boulder 49 Southwest in a. 1930 (photo Harold Colton, copyright Museum of Northern Arizona; DVD1843) and b. 2004 (photo Wesley Bernardini; DVD1162); see also DVD1161-1171, 1883, 2164-2166, 2422-2424, and 2529-2530.

a.

b.

Figure I.16. Example of vandalism: Boulder 55 West in a. 1930 (photo Harold Colton, copyright Museum of Northern Arizona; DVD1847) and b. 2004 (photo Wesley Bernardini; DVD1285); see also DVD1284-1306, 1844-1848, 2002, 2173-2175, 2434-2438, and 2536-2538.

a.

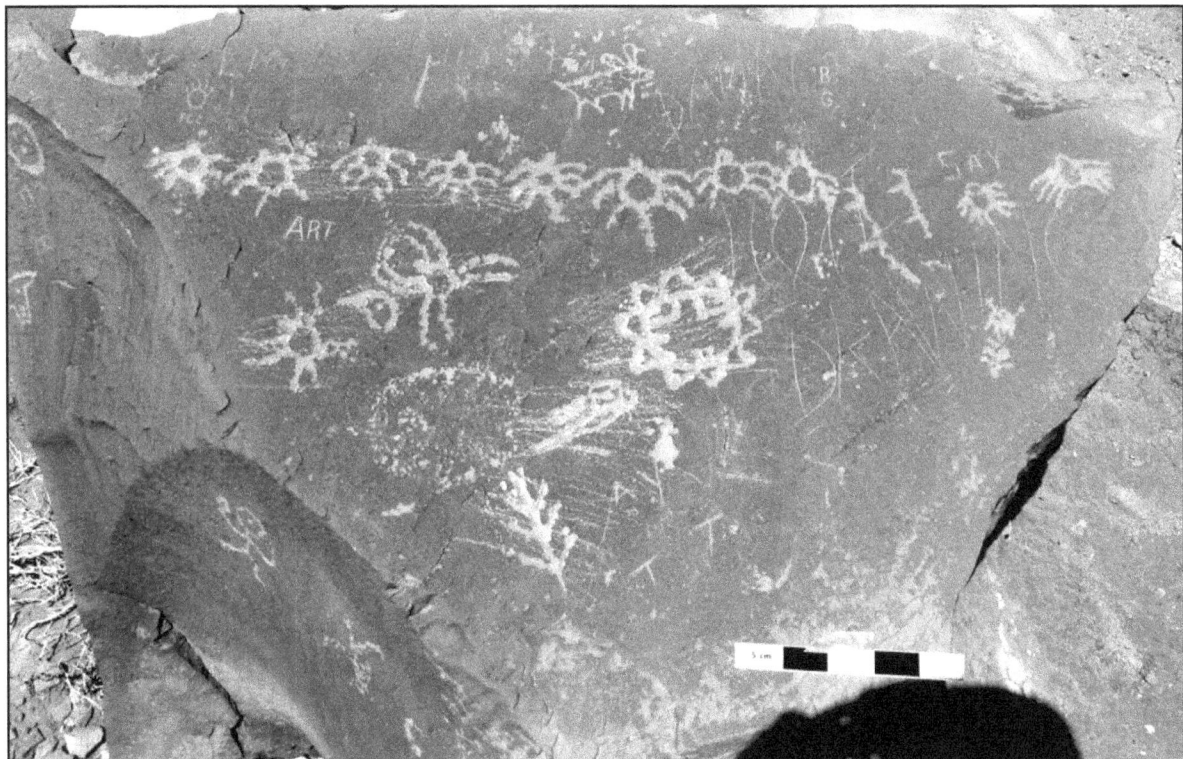

b.

Figure I.17. Example of vandalism: Boulder 60 Top in a. 1978 (photo Helen Michaelis, copyright UCLA Rock Art Archive; DVD1891) and b. 2004 (photo Wesley Bernardini; DVD1346); see also DVD1345-1355, 1891, 2003, 2079, 2176, 2442-2443, 2445, and 2541.

a.

b.

Figure I.18. Example of vandalism: Boulder 17 Northwest in a. 1930 (photo Harold Colton, copyright Museum of Northern Arizona; DVD1811) and b. 2004 (photo Wesley Bernardini; DVD0329). In text as Figure 3.6; see also DVD0325-0369, 1810-1811, 1902, 1982, 2027-2028, 2132, and 2295.

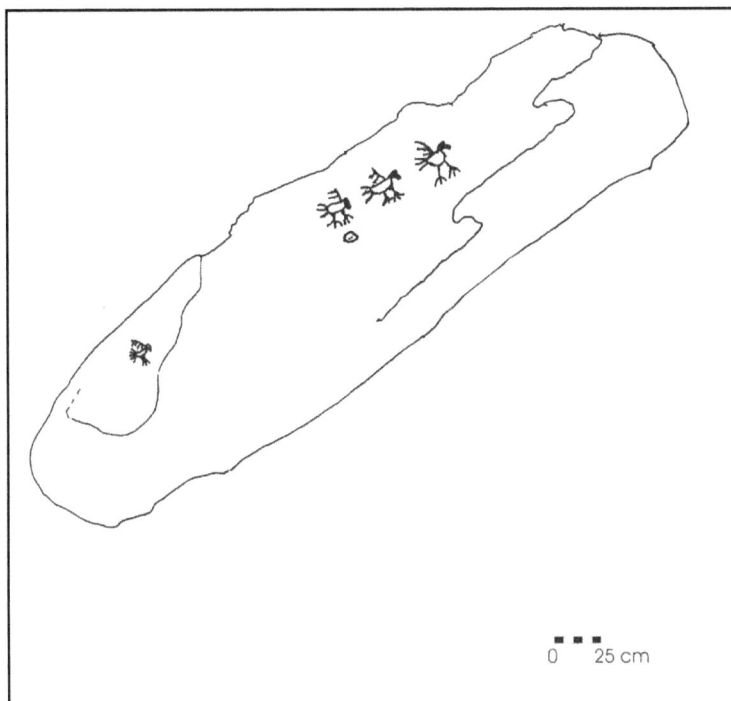

Figure I.19. Boulder 9 Southeast (reconstructed using 1998 photographs); see DVD0123-0143, 1852, 1900, 2125, and 2253-2256.

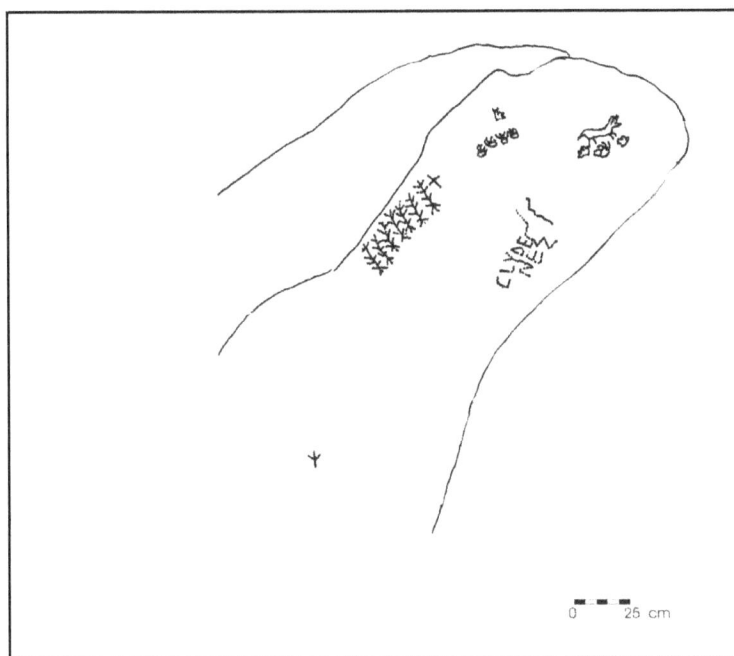

Figure I.20. Boulder 12 Southwest (reconstructed using 1978 photographs); see DVD0171-0196, 1853, 1901, 2015, 2088-2089, 2266-2268, and 2479.

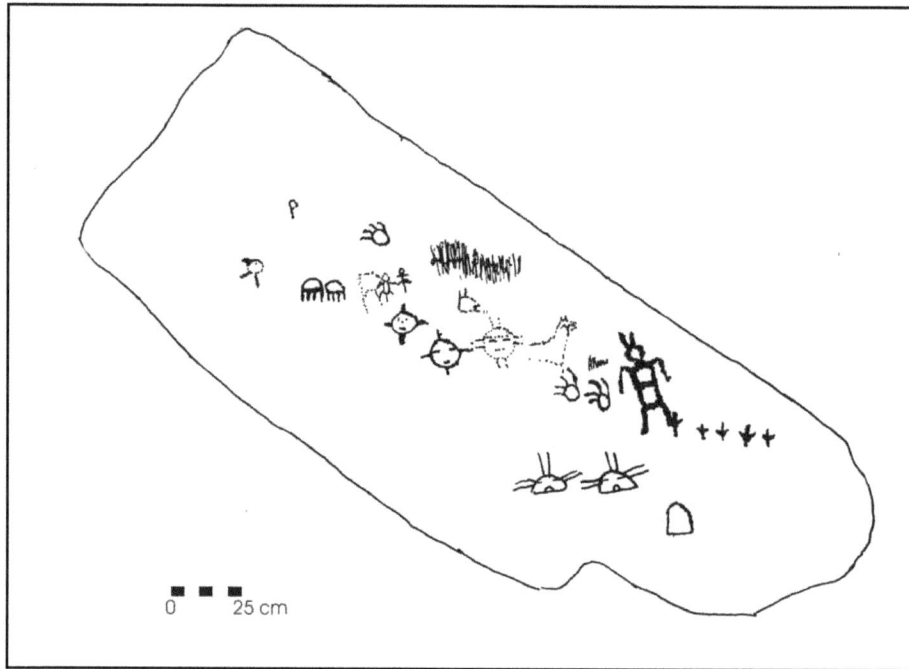

Figure I.21. Boulder 13 Northeast (reconstructed using 1930 photographs); see DVD0197-0224, 1808, 1978-1979, 2016-2017, 2127, 2269-2274.

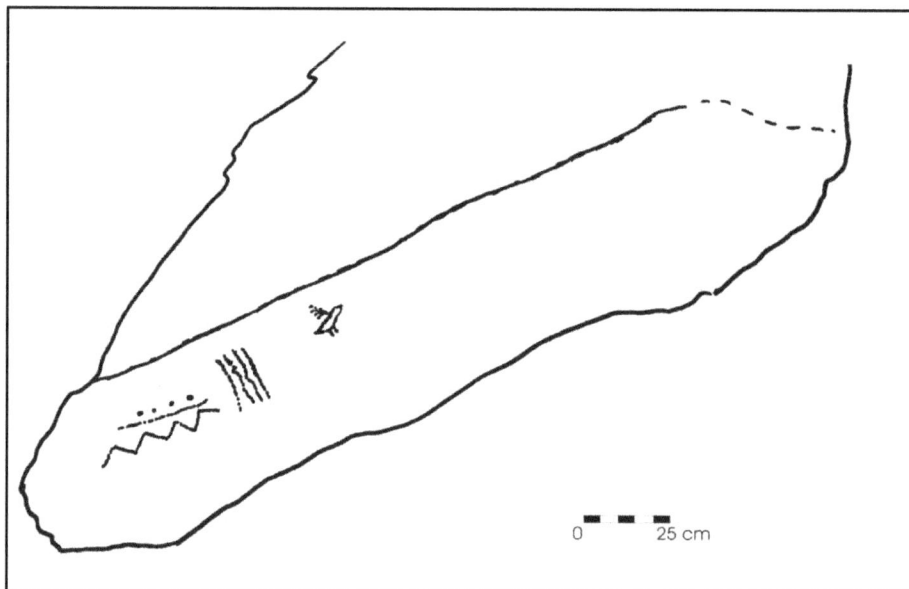

Figure I.22. Boulder 13 Southwest (reconstructed using 1998 photographs); see DVD0233-0241, 2128, and 2279.

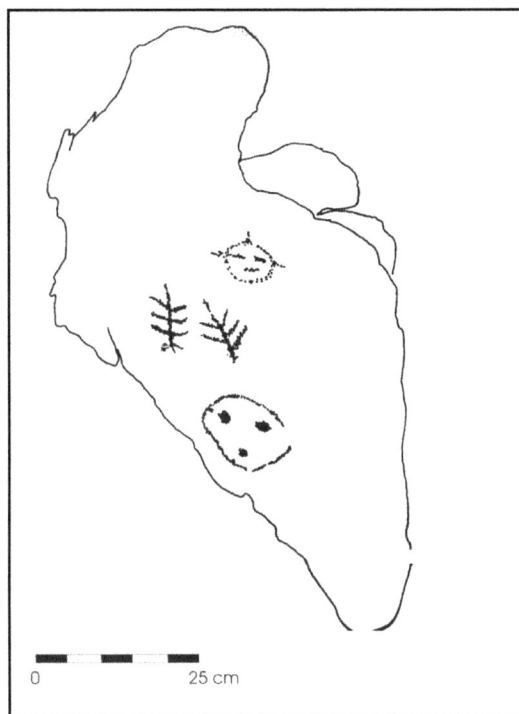

Figure I.23. Boulder 13 Top; see DVD0242-0249.

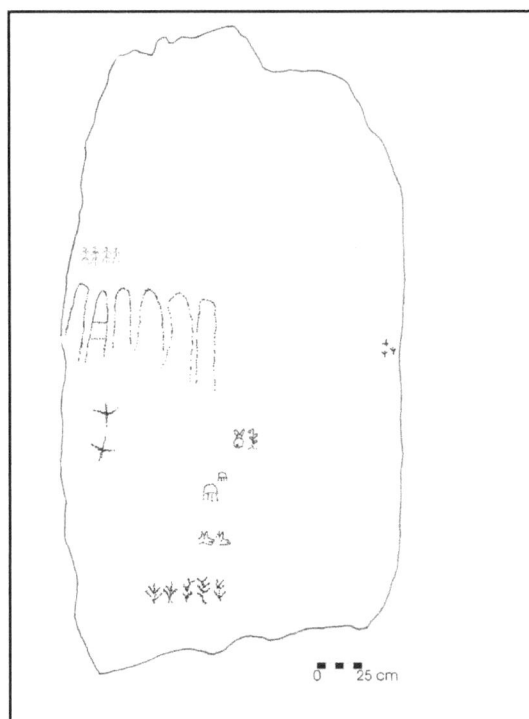

Figure I.24. Boulder 14 East (reconstructed using 1984 photographs); see DVD0254-0263, 2018-2022, and 2480-2481.

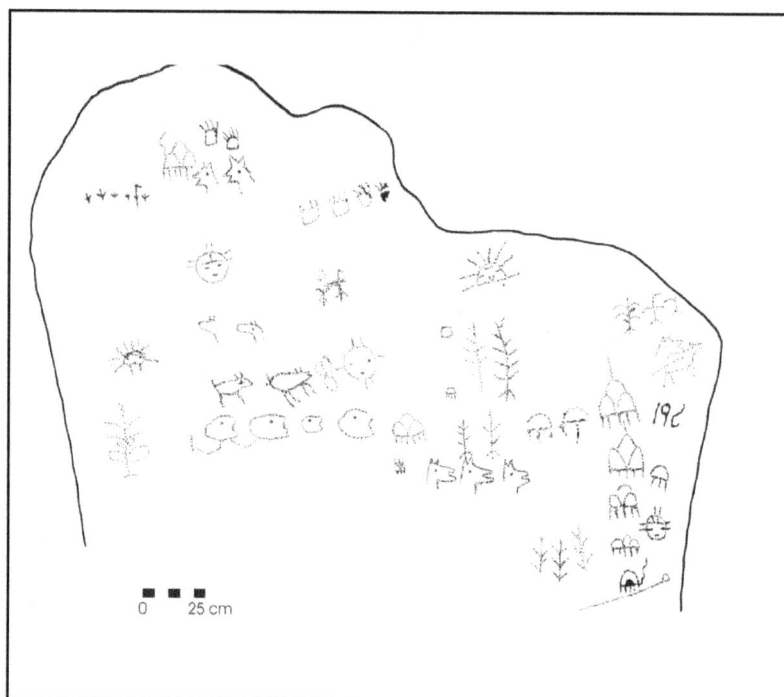

Figure I.25. Boulder 14 Nouth (reconstructed using 1930 photographs); see DVD0264-0281, 1809, 1854, 2023, 2104-2105, and 2280-2282.

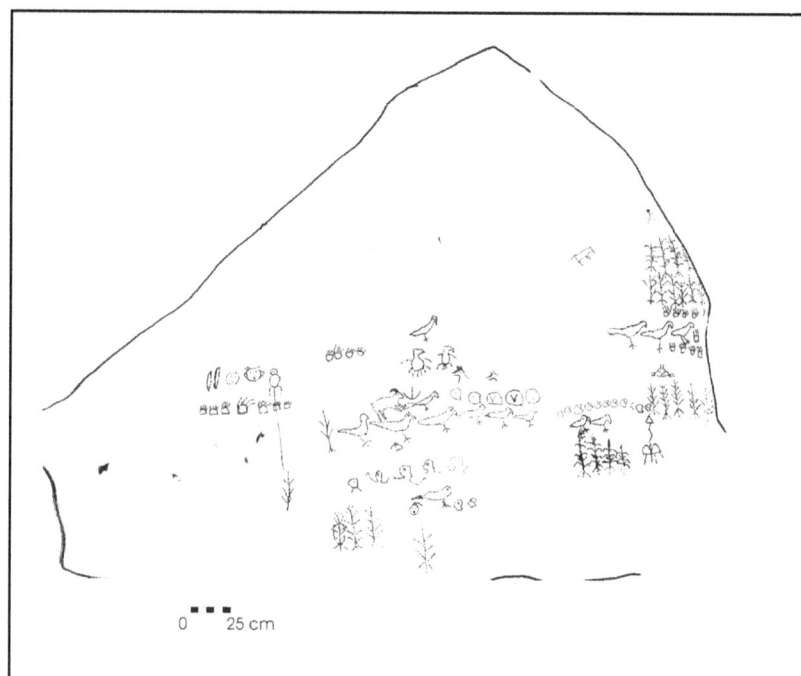

Figure I.26. Boulder 14 South (reconstructed using 1930 photographs); see DVD0282-0305, 1855, 1980-1981, 2024-2026, 2090, 2094-2095, 2106-2108, 2129-2131, 2283-2294, and 2482-2483.

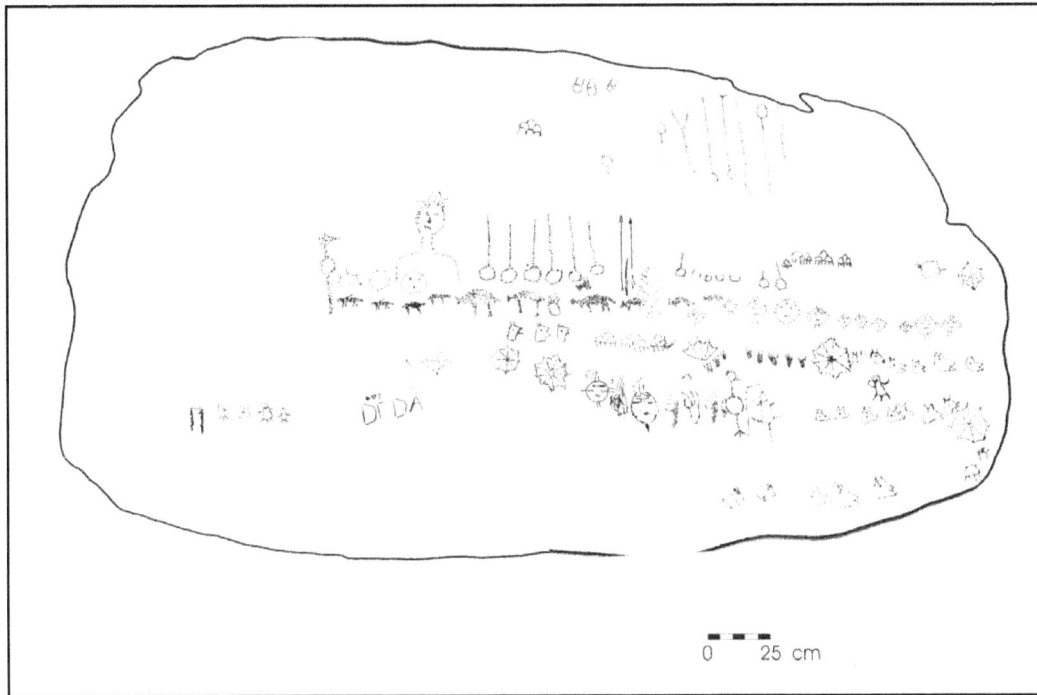

Figure I.27. Boulder 17 Northwest (reconstructed using 1930 photographs); see DVD0325-0369, 1810-1811, 1902, 1982, 2027-2028, 2132, and 2295.

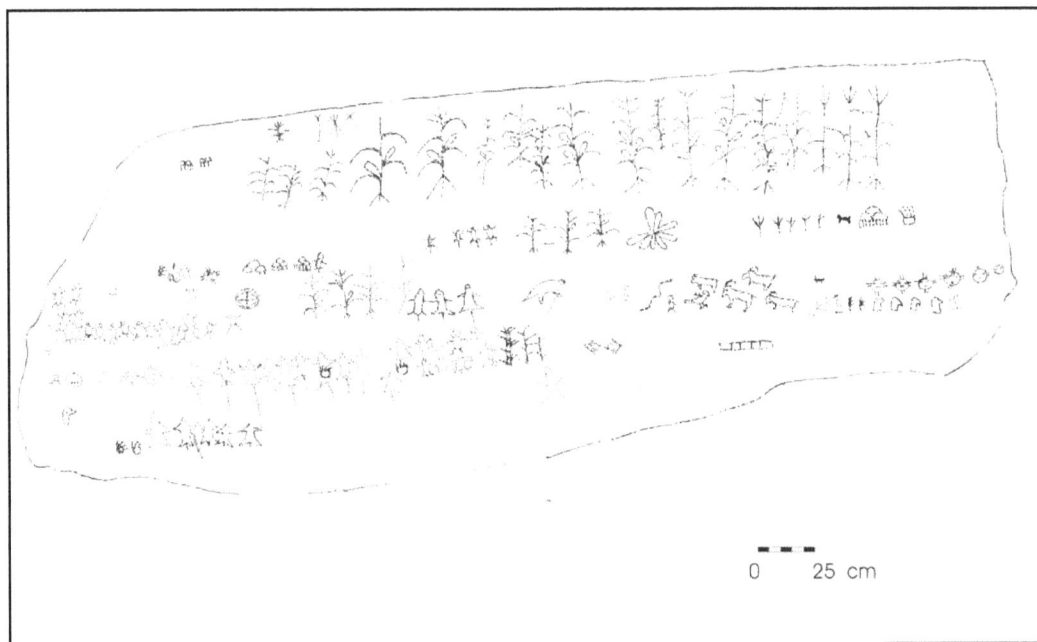

Figure I.28. Boulder 17 South (reconstructed using 1930 photographs); see DVD0370-0388, 1812-1815, 1856-1857, 1903-1904, 1983, 2029-2030, 2096, 2109-2110, 2133-2134, and 2296-2302.

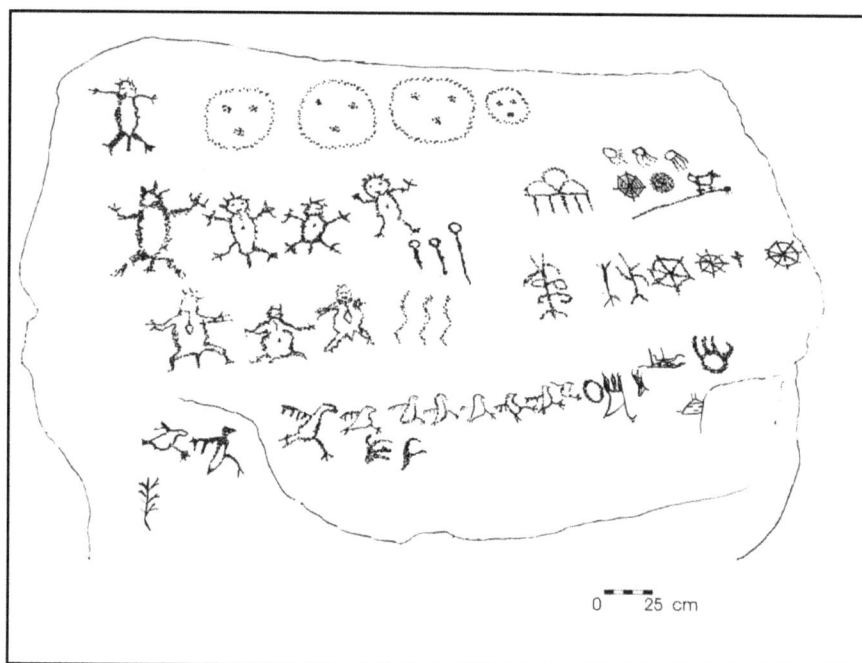

Figure I.29. Boulder 17 Southeast (reconstructed using 1930 photographs); see DVD0389-0409, 2031-2033, 2135, 2303-2309, and 2484.

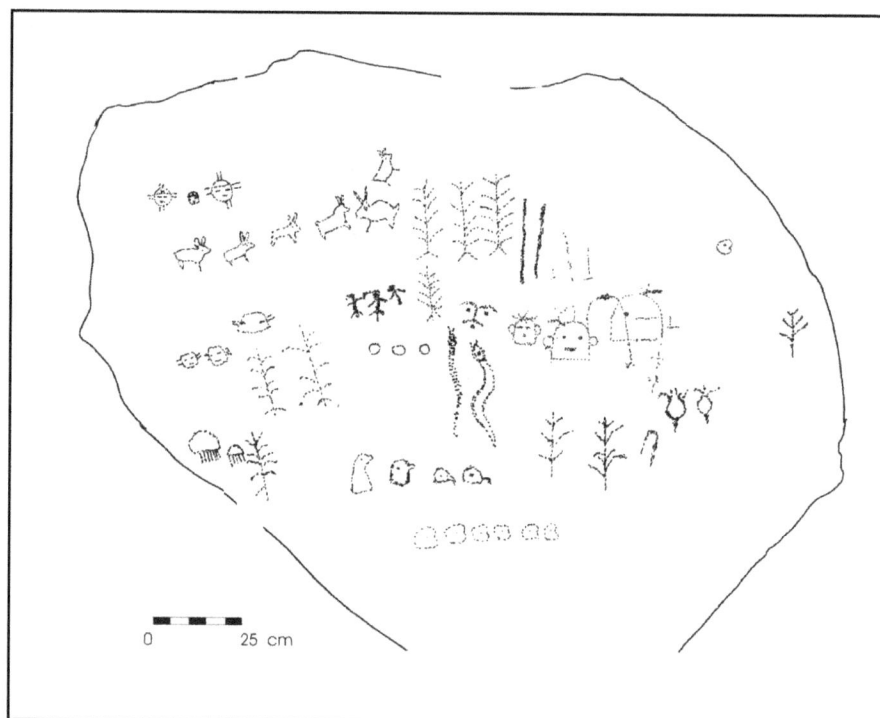

Figure I.30. Boulder 18 North (reconstructed using 1930 photographs); see DVD0426-0444, 1817, 2136, and 2310-2311.

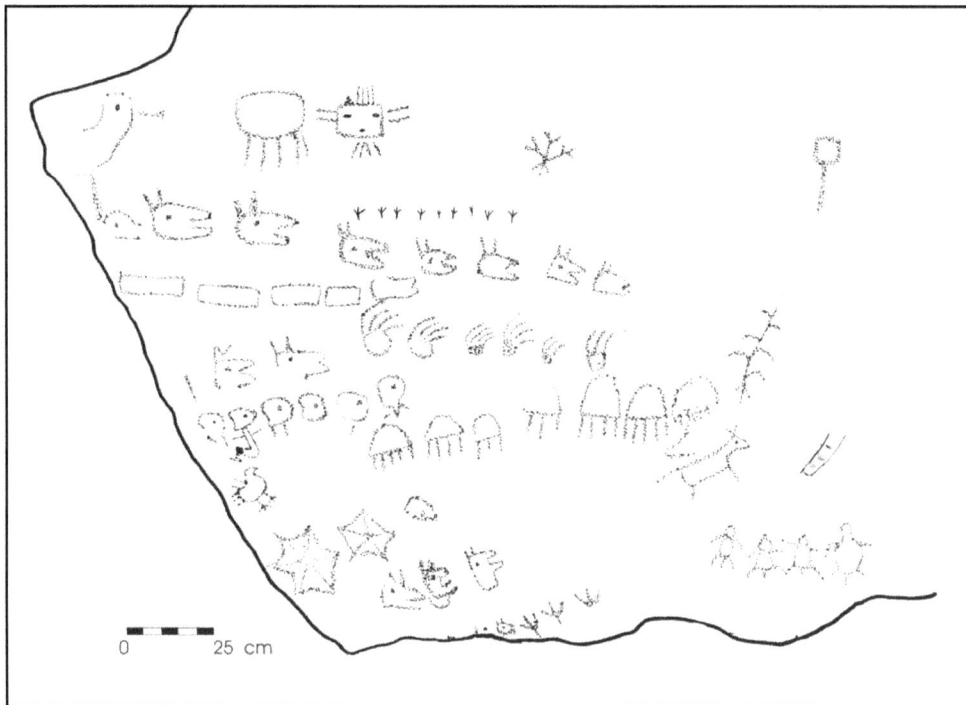

Figure I.31. Boulder 18 South, bottom half (reconstructed using 1930 photographs); see DVD0446, 0449-0456, 1905, 2312, and 2314.

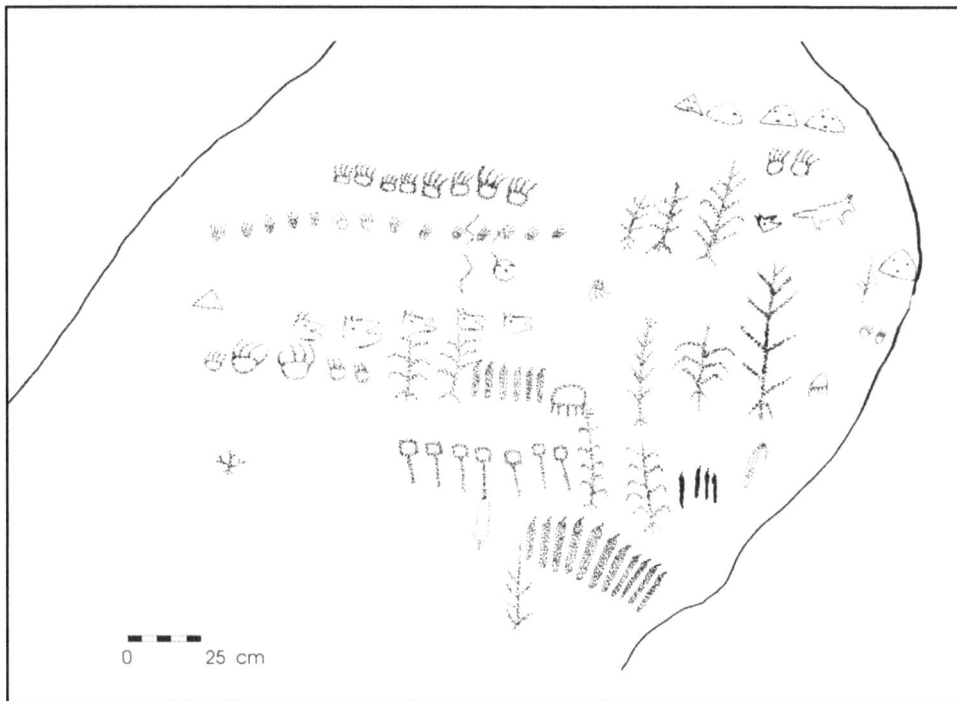

Figure I.32. Boulder 18 South, top half (reconstructed using 1930 photographs); see DVD0447, 0457-0465, 1818, 2313, and 2316-2317.

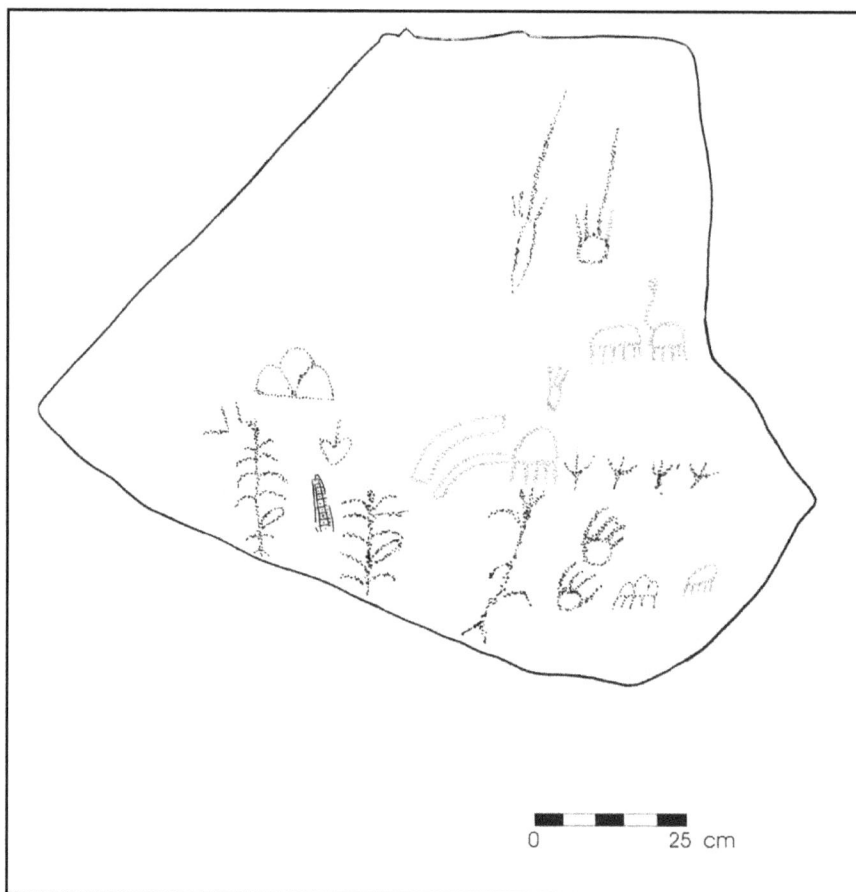

Figure I.33. Boulder 18 Southwest (reconstructed using 1930 photographs); see DVD0468-0480, 1819, 2319, and 2320.

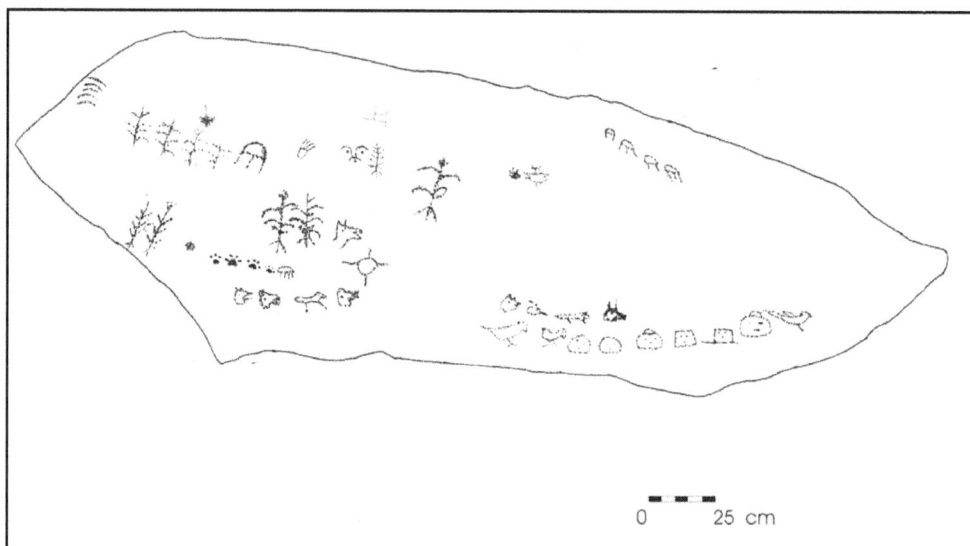

Figure I.34. Boulder 18 Top (reconstructed using 1930 photographs); see DVD0411-0425, 1820, 2034, 2111, 2137, and 2321-2325.

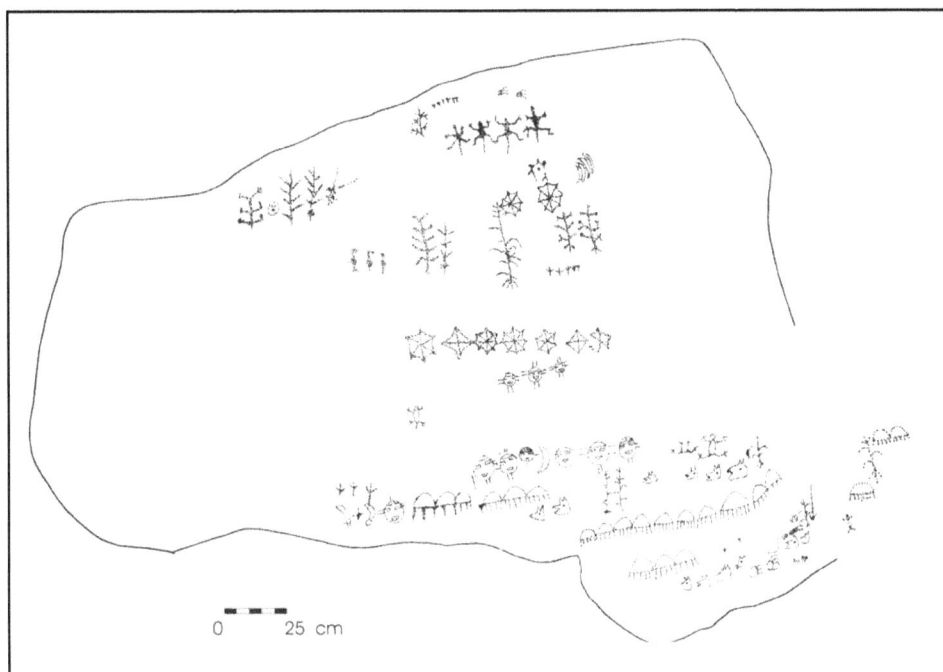

Figure I.35. Boulder 18 West (reconstructed using 1930 photographs); see DVD0487-0505, 1821-1823, 1860, 1906-9109, 1984, 2035-2036, 2112-2113, 2138-2139, and 2326-2333.

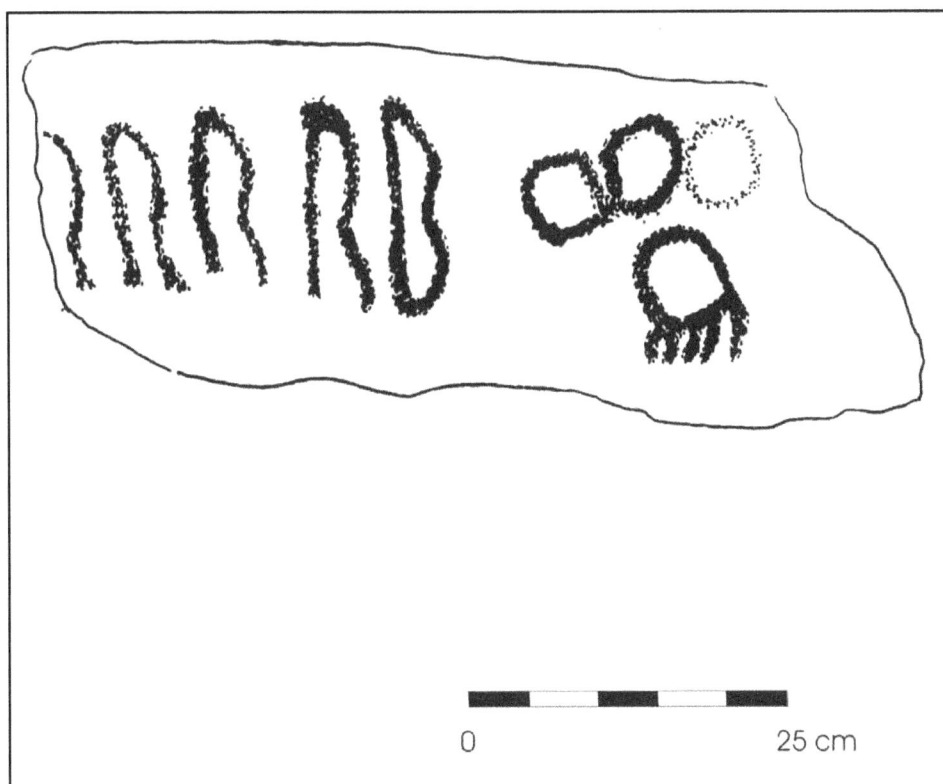

Figure I.36. Boulder 30 North (reconstructed using 1978 photographs); see DVD0550-0553, and 2336.

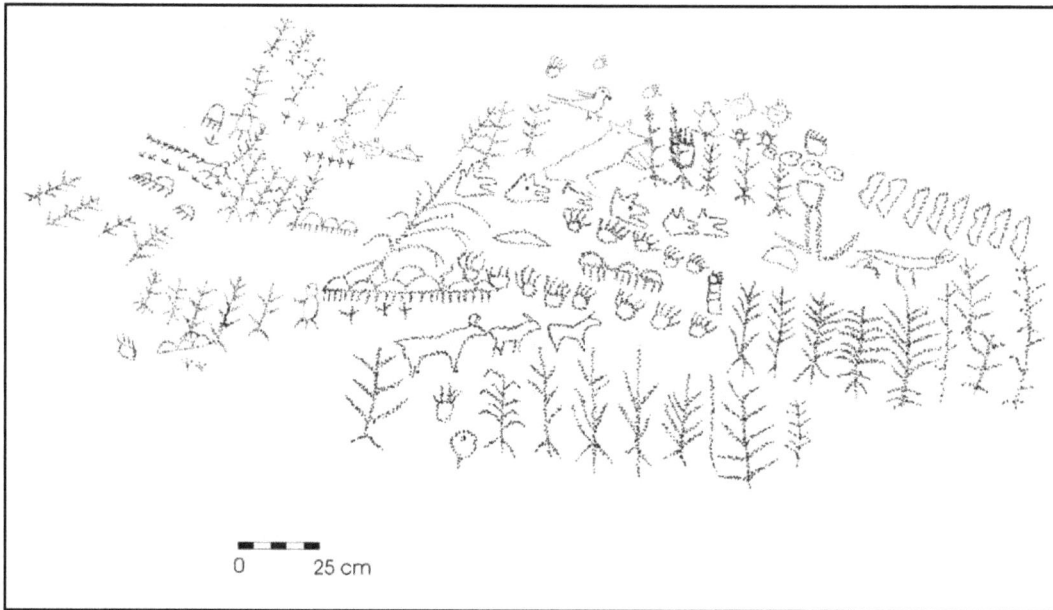

Figure I.37. Boulder 30 South (reconstructed using 1930 photographs); see DVD0554-0579, 1824-1828, 1911-1914, 1987, 2040-2043, 2091, 2114, 2140-2142, 2337-2354, 2485-2488, and 2557-2558.

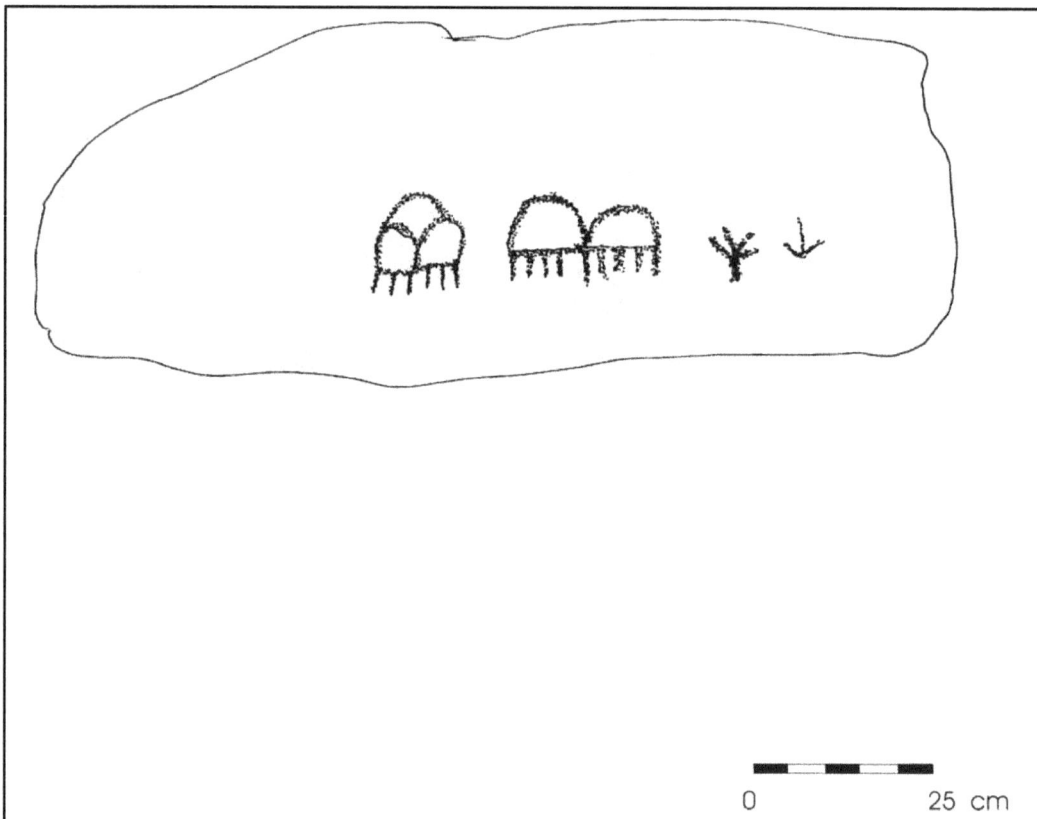

Figure I.38. Boulder 31 East; see DVD0585-0587

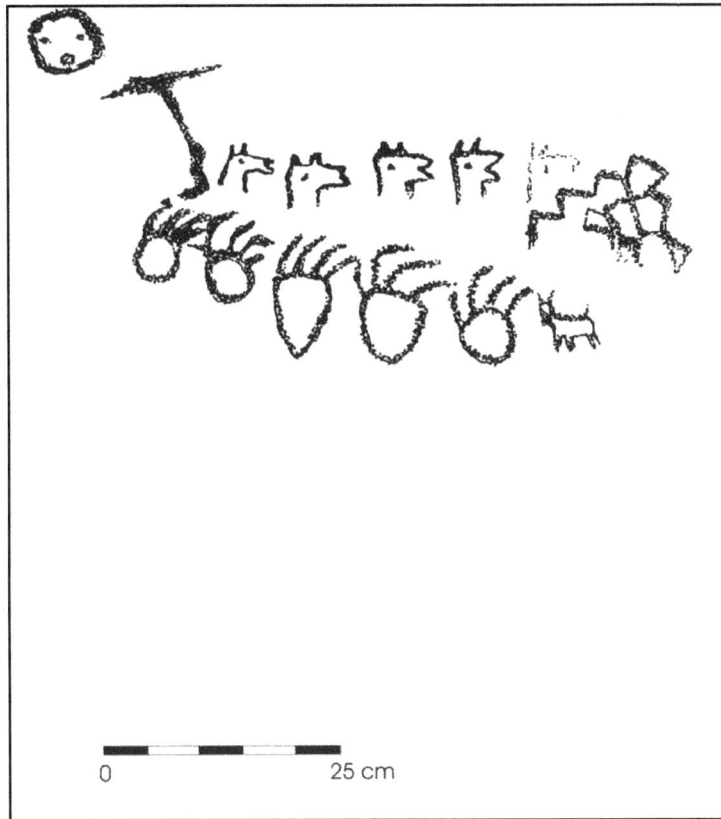

Figure I.39. Boulder 32 Southwest; see DVD0598-0599.

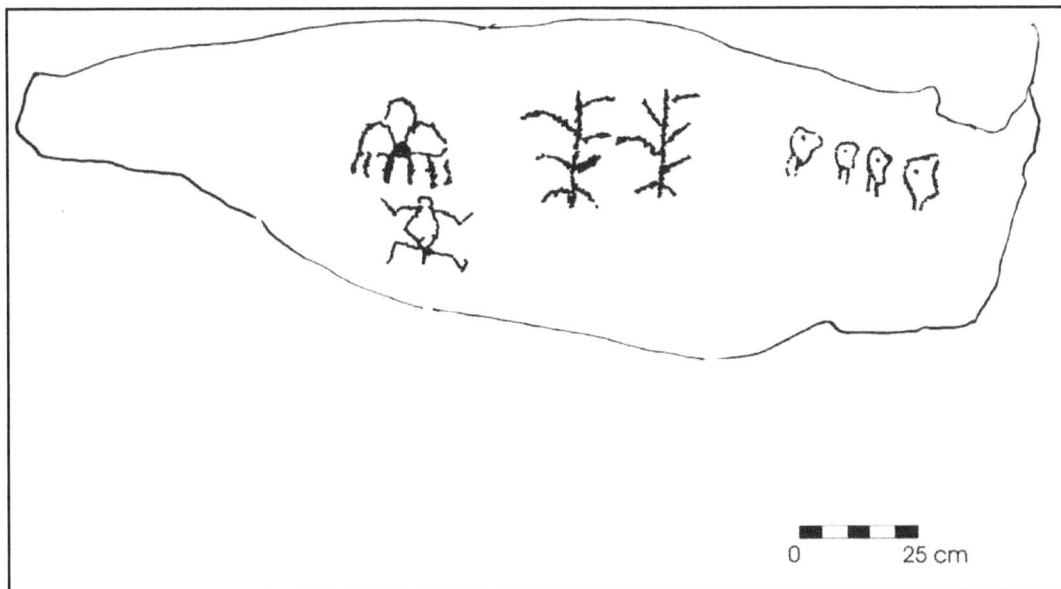

Figure I.40. Boulder 33 North (reconstructed using 1978 photographs); see DVD0600-0605, 1865, and 2355.

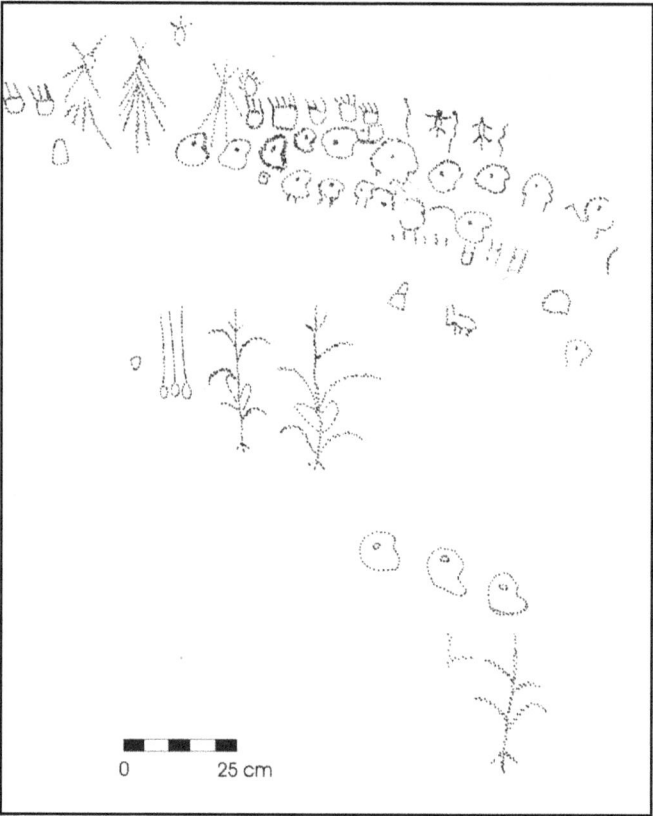

Figure I.41. Boulder 33 Top (reconstructed using 1984 photographs); see DVD0606-0615.

Figure I.42. Boulder 34 East; see DVD0616-0620.

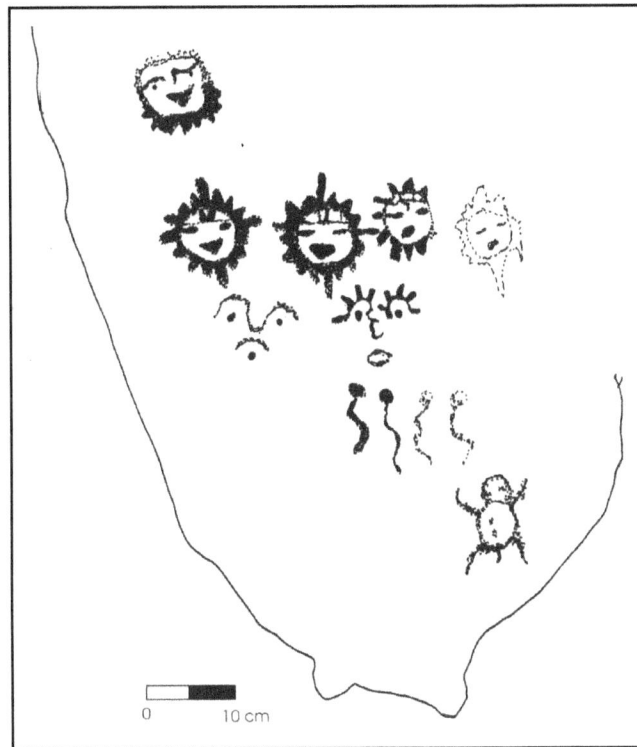

Figure I.43. Boulder 34 North (reconstructed using 1978 photographs); see DVD0621-0632, 1866, and 1988-1989.

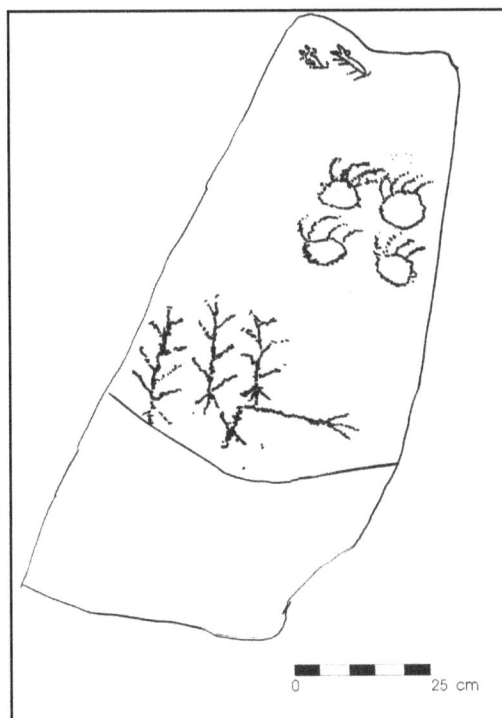

Figure I.44. Boulder 34 South (reconstructed using 1978 photographs); see DVD0633-0638, 1867, 1915-1916, 2356-2360, and 2489-2490.

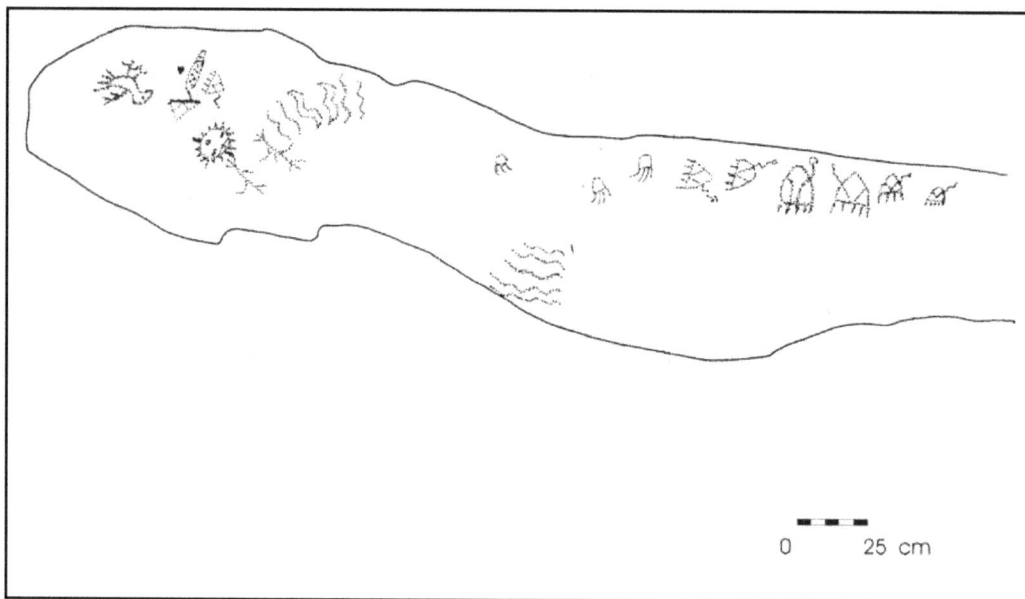

Figure I.45. Boulder 34 Top (reconstructed using 1984 photographs); see DVD0639-0648, 1990, 2044-2047, 2144-2145, and 2361.

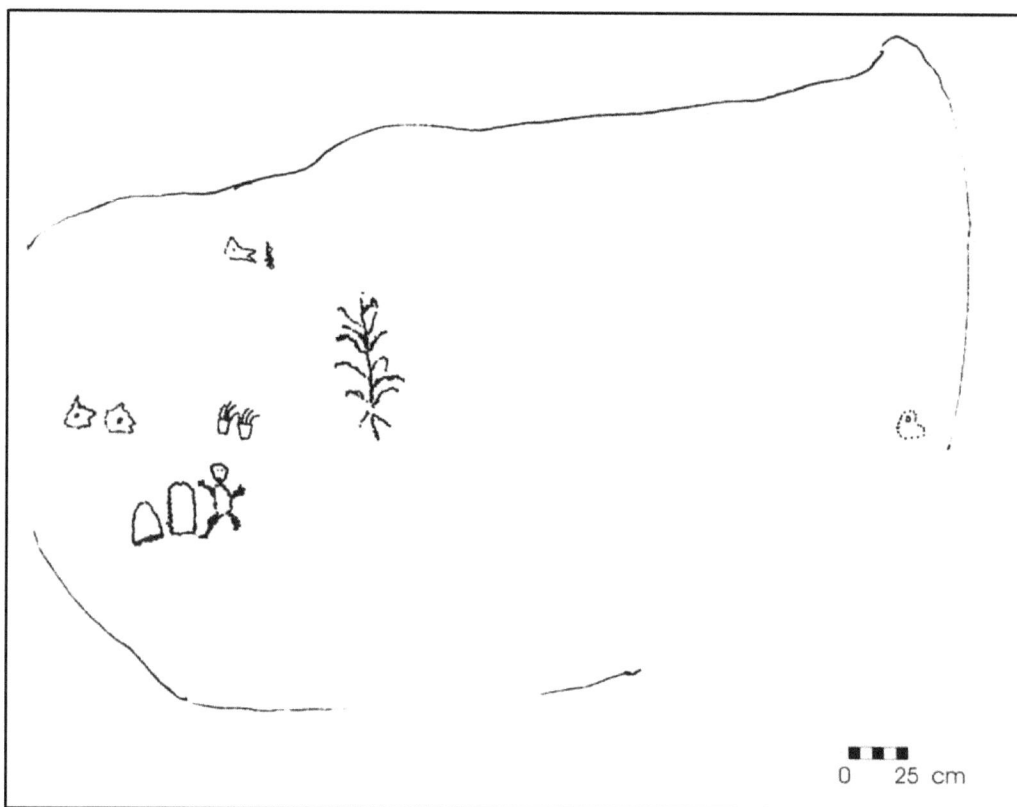

Figure I.46. Boulder 34 West; see DVD0659-0668, 2146-2147, and 2362.

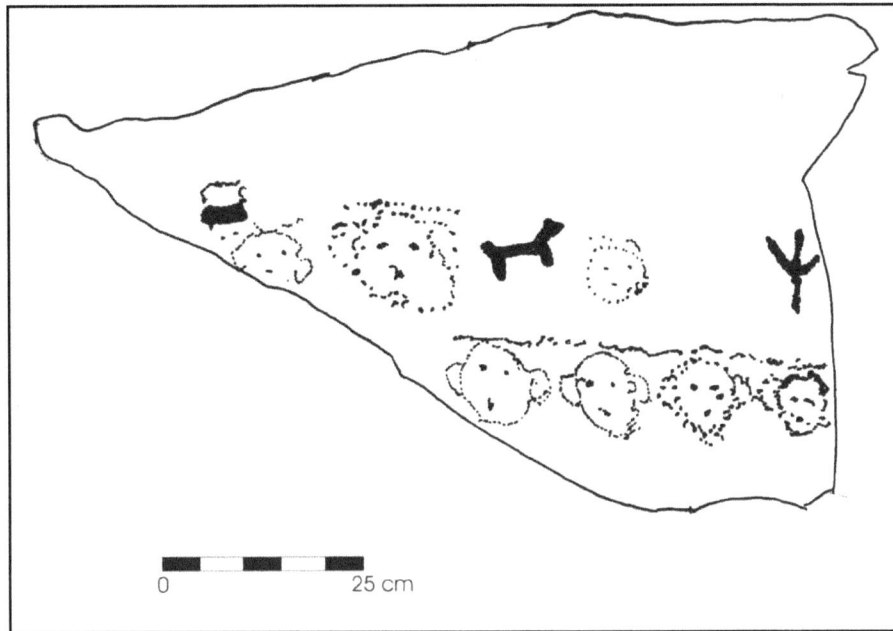

Figure I.47. Boulder 35 East; see DVD0669-0679.

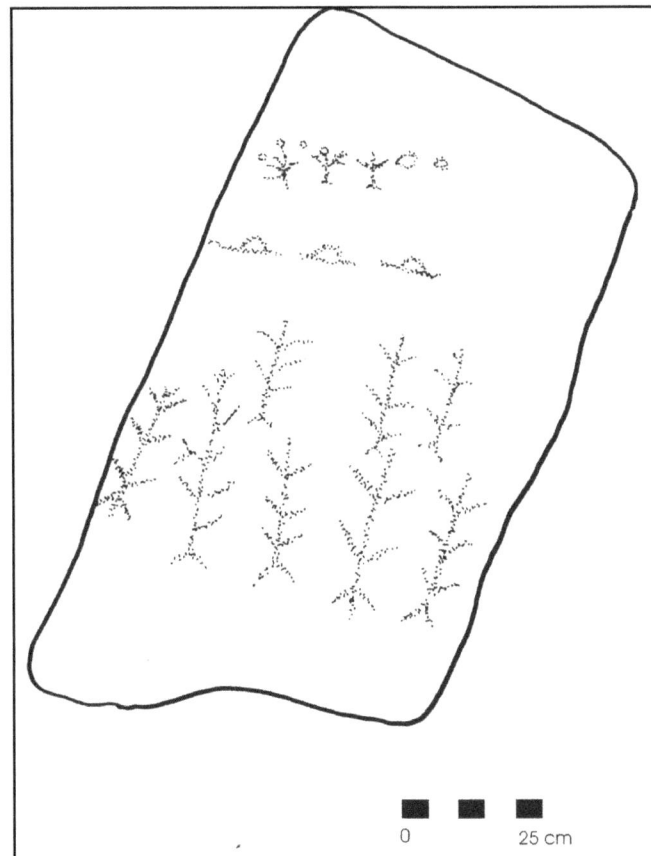

Figure I.48. Boulder 35 South (reconstructed using 1978 photographs); see DVD0685-0695, 1868, 1917-1918, 2364-2368, and 2491-2492.

Figure I.49. Boulder 35 Top (reconstructed using 1930 photographs); see DVD0696-0715, 1829-1830, 1919-1920, 2092, 2363, 2369-2370, and 2493-2498.

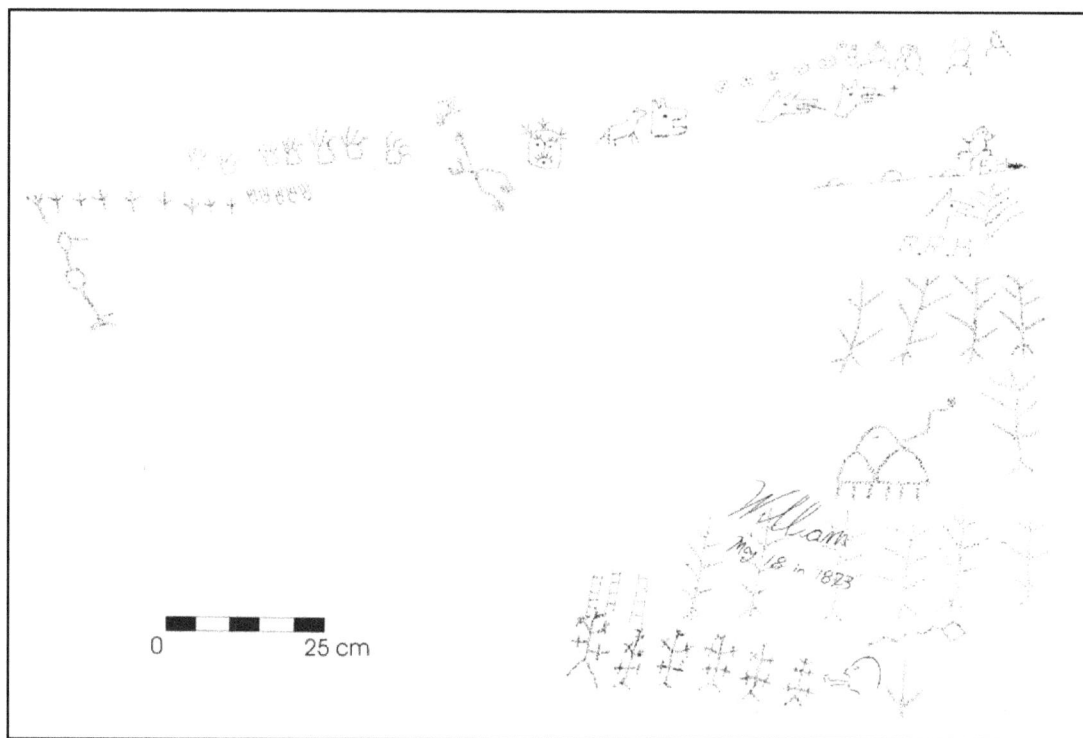

Figure I.50. Boulder 35 West; see DVD0716-0744.

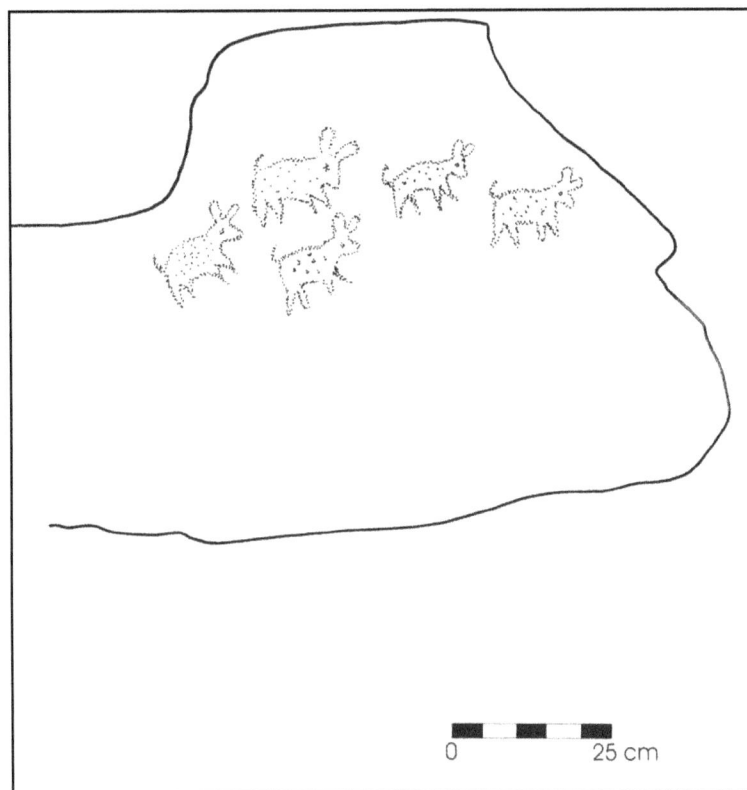

Figure I.51. Boulder 36 East (reconstructed using 1930 photographs); see DVD0745-0746, 1831, 1869, 1921, and 2371-2373.

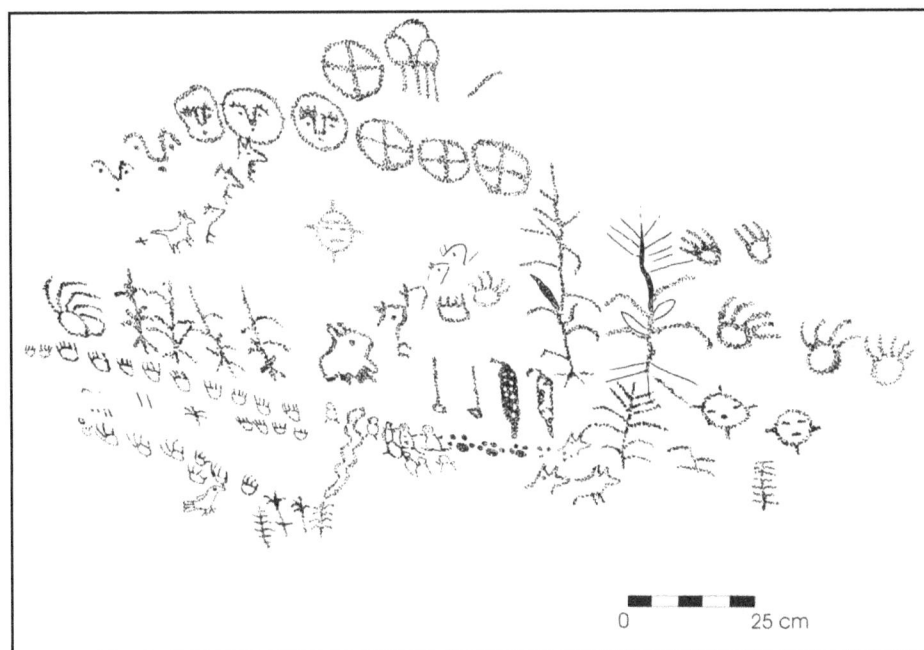

Figure I.52. Boulder 37 Top (reconstructed using 1930 photographs); see DVD0749-0767, 1832, 1870, 1922-1923, 1991, 2097, 2148, 2374-2380, and 2499.

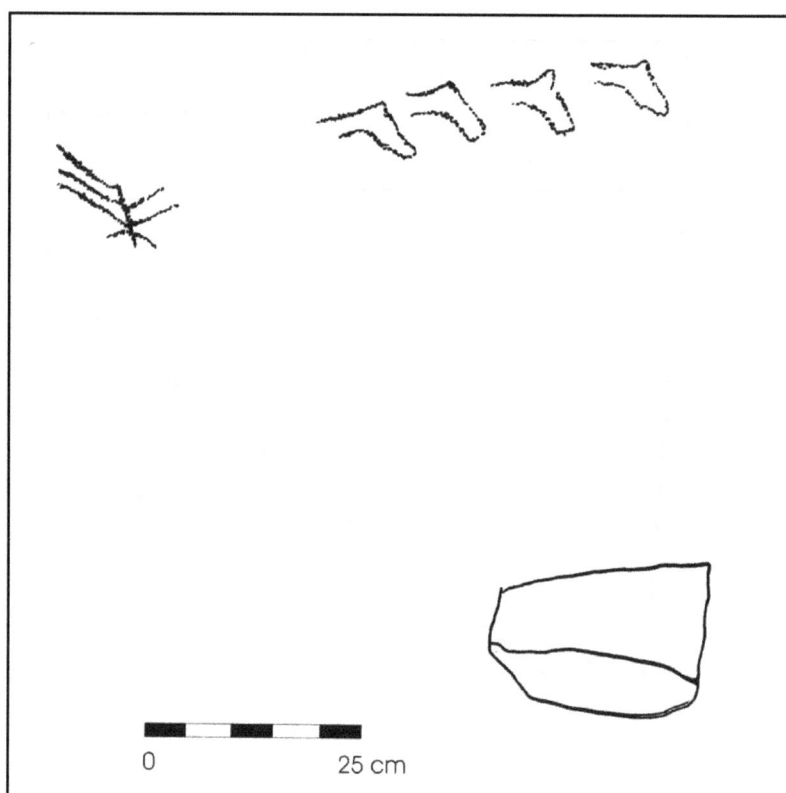

Figure I.53. Boulder 38 South; see DVD0768-0773.

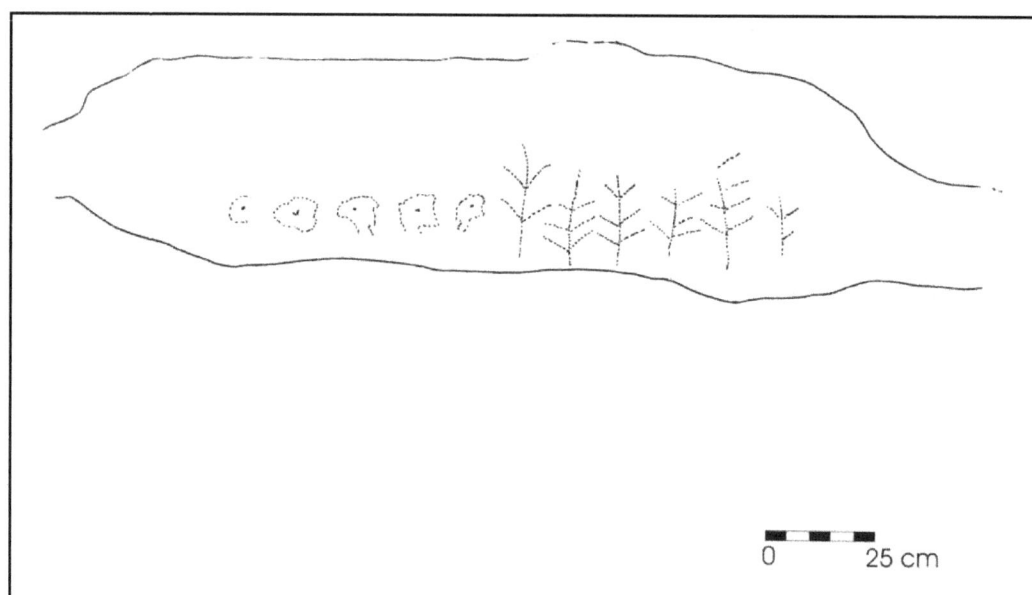

Figure I.54. Boulder 39 North; see DVD0779-0783.

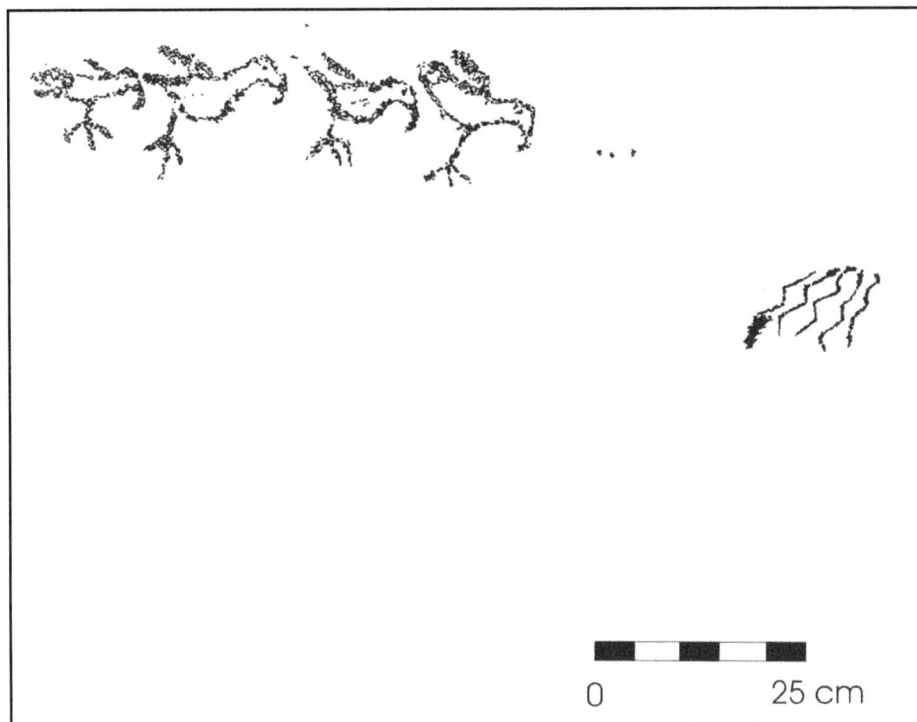

Figure I.55. Boulder 40 East (reconstructed using 1930 photographs); see DVD0789-0792, 1833, 1871-1872, 1924, 1992-1993, 2049-2050, and 2381.

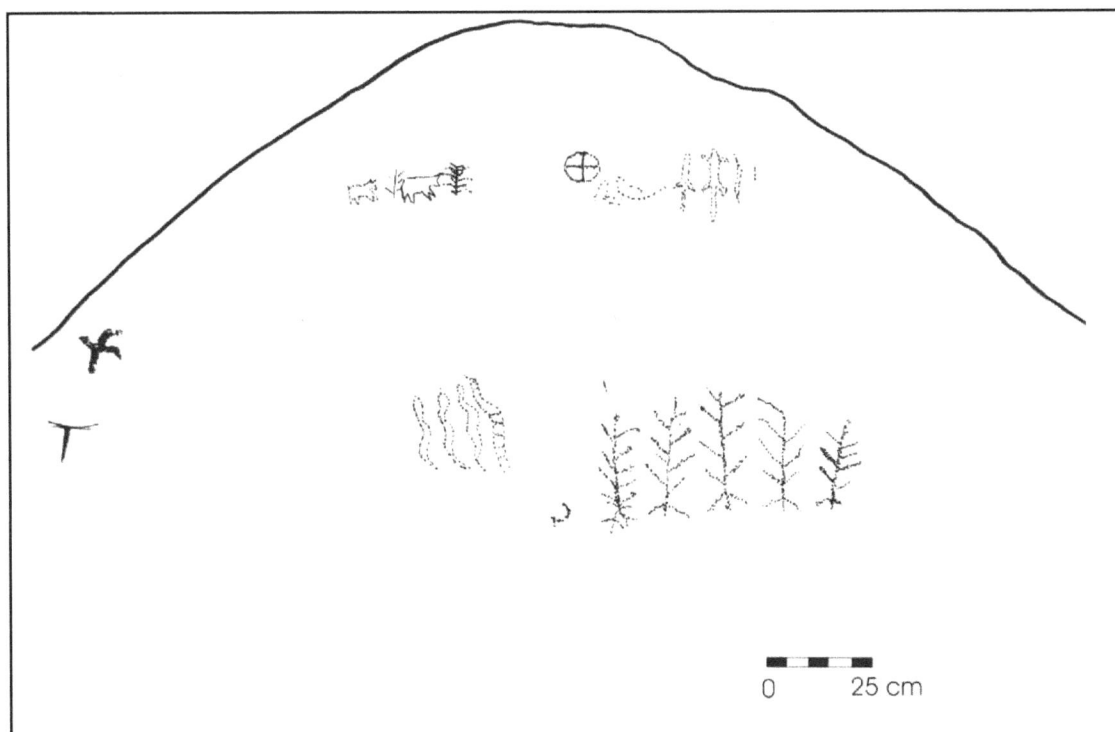

Figure I.56. Boulder 40 South; see DVD0793-0799, and 2382-2383.

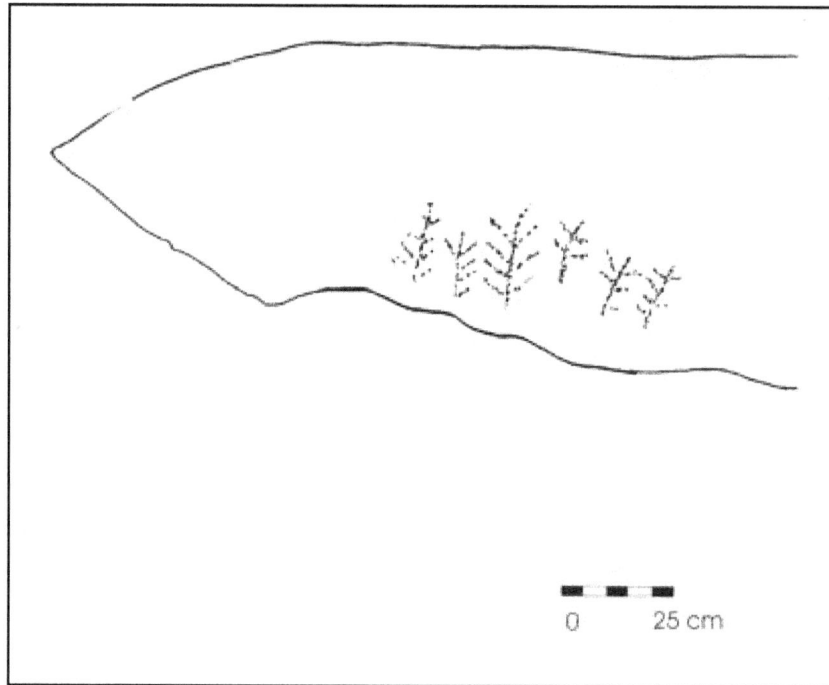

Figure I.57. Boulder 41 Top; see DVD0800-0802.

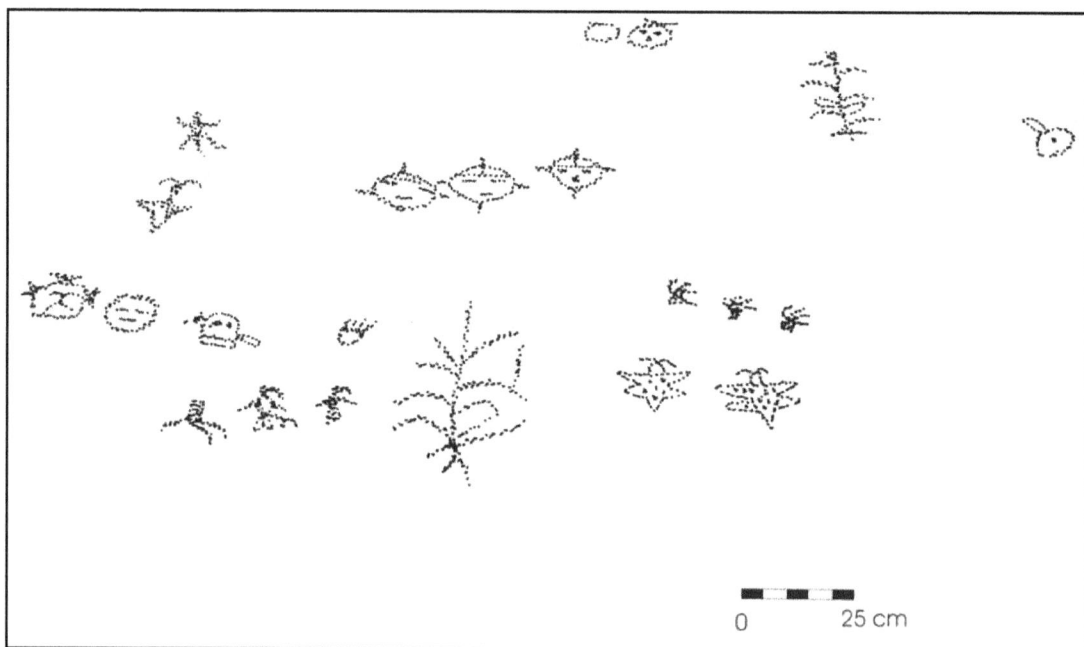

Figure I.58. Boulder 43 South (reconstructed using 1930 photographs); see DVD0808-0822, 1834, 1873, 1994, 2051, 2098, 2149-2151, 2384-2389, and 2500-2502.

Figure I.59. Boulder 44 Top; see DVD0823-0833.

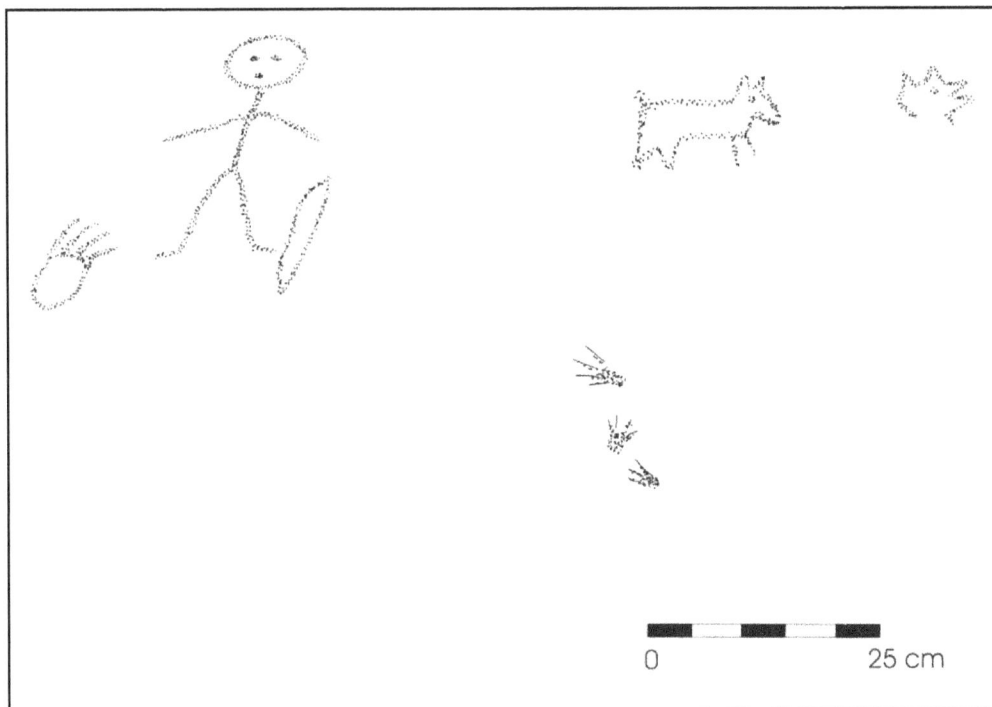

Figure I.60. Boulder 45 Top (reconstructed using 1978 photographs); see DVD0837-0849, 1874, 1995, 2052, 2390, and 2503-2505.

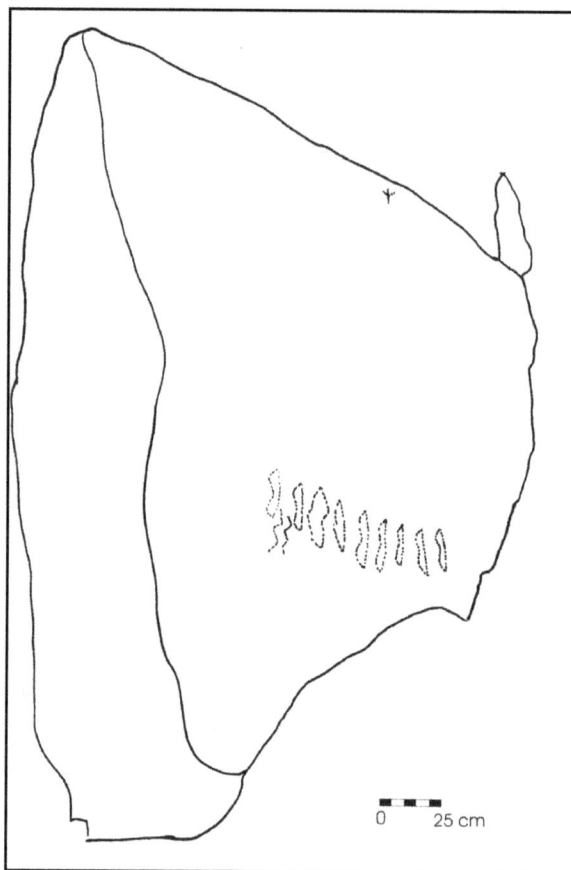

Figure I.61. Boulder 46 West (reconstructed using 1978 photographs); see DVD0853-0858, 1875, 2053, 2152, 2391, and 2506-2507.

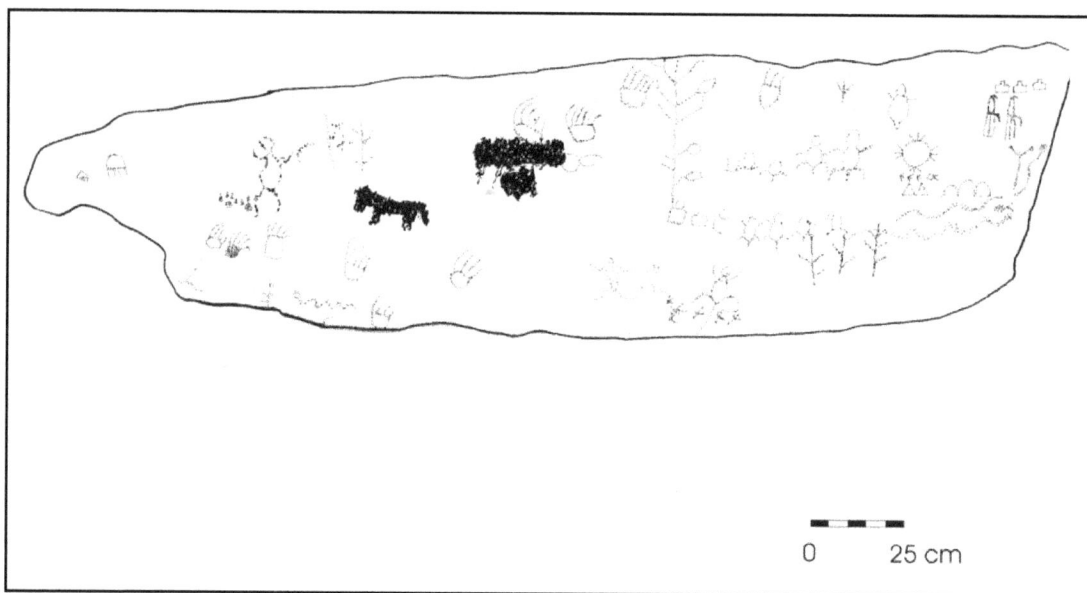

Figure I.62. Boulder 48 Northeast, lower left (reconstructed using 1930 photographs); see DVD0866-0867, 0871-0874, 0877, 0913, 0917, 0922-0923, 0929-0930, 1836, 1925, and 2509.

Figure I.63. Boulder 48 Northeast, lower right (reconstructed using 1930 photographs); see DVD0868, 0876, 0915, 0919, and 1835.

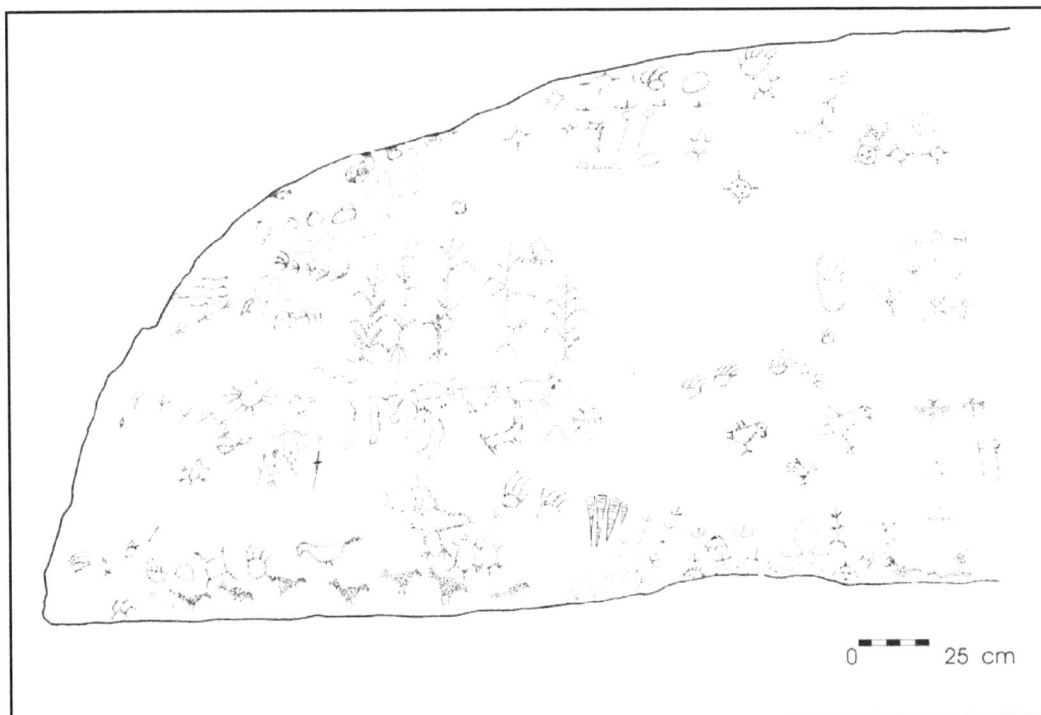

Figure I.64. Boulder 48 Northeast, upper left (reconstructed using 1930 photographs); see DVD0865, 0875, 0879-0901, 0907, 0914, 0918, 0924, 0931-0936, and 2508-2509.

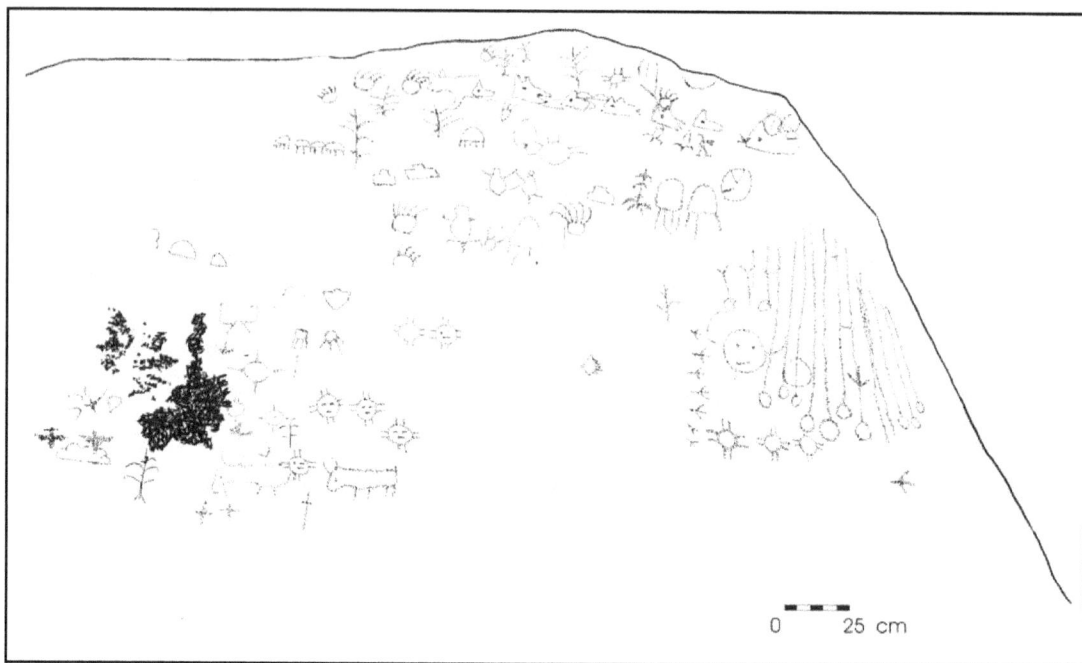

Figure I.65. Boulder 48 Northeast, upper right (reconstructed using 1930 photographs); see DVD0861-0863, 0902, 0909-0910, 0916, 0920-0921, 0937-0938, and 1926-1927.

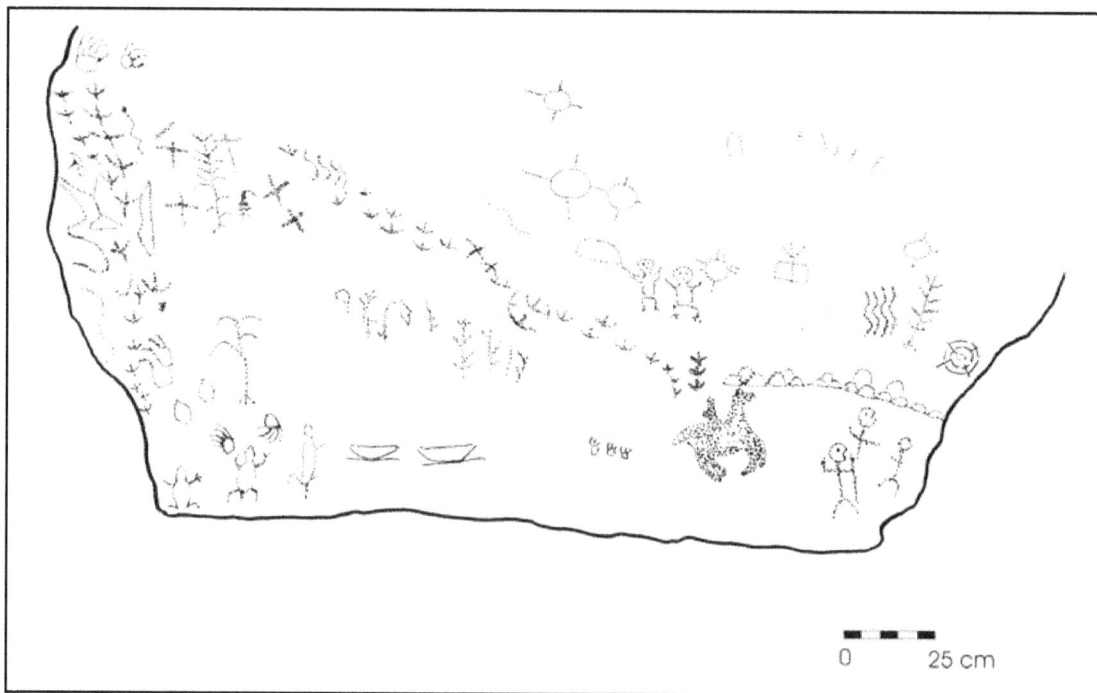

Figure I.66. Boulder 48 Northwest, bottom half (reconstructed using 1930 photographs); see DVD0940-0943, 0945-0949, 0951-0952, 0954-0956, 0958, 0970-0972, 1876, and 2153-2154.

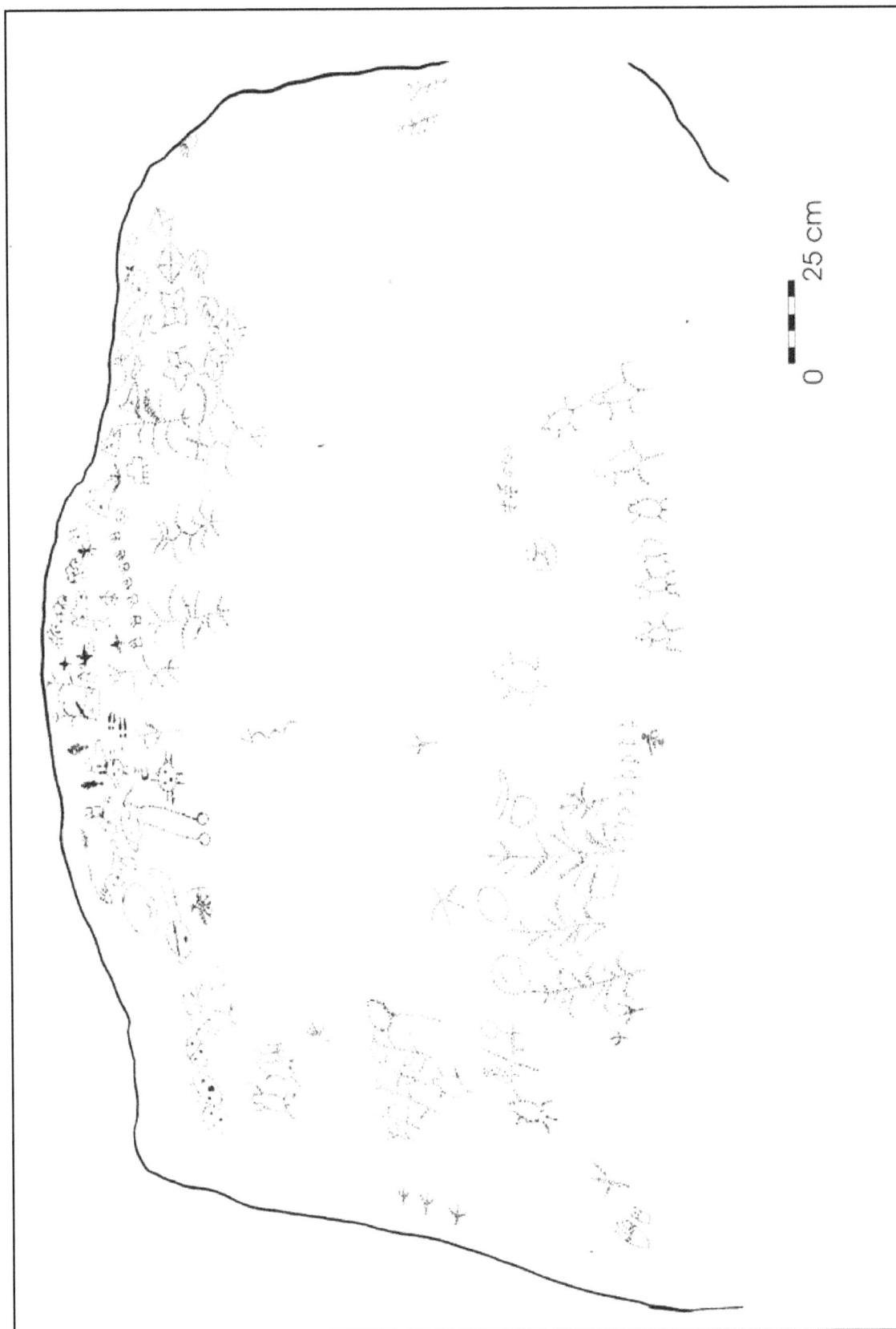

Figure I.67. Boulder 48 Northwest, top half (reconstructed using 1930 photographs); see DVD0944, 0953, 0957, 0959-0969, 0973, 1928, and 2559.

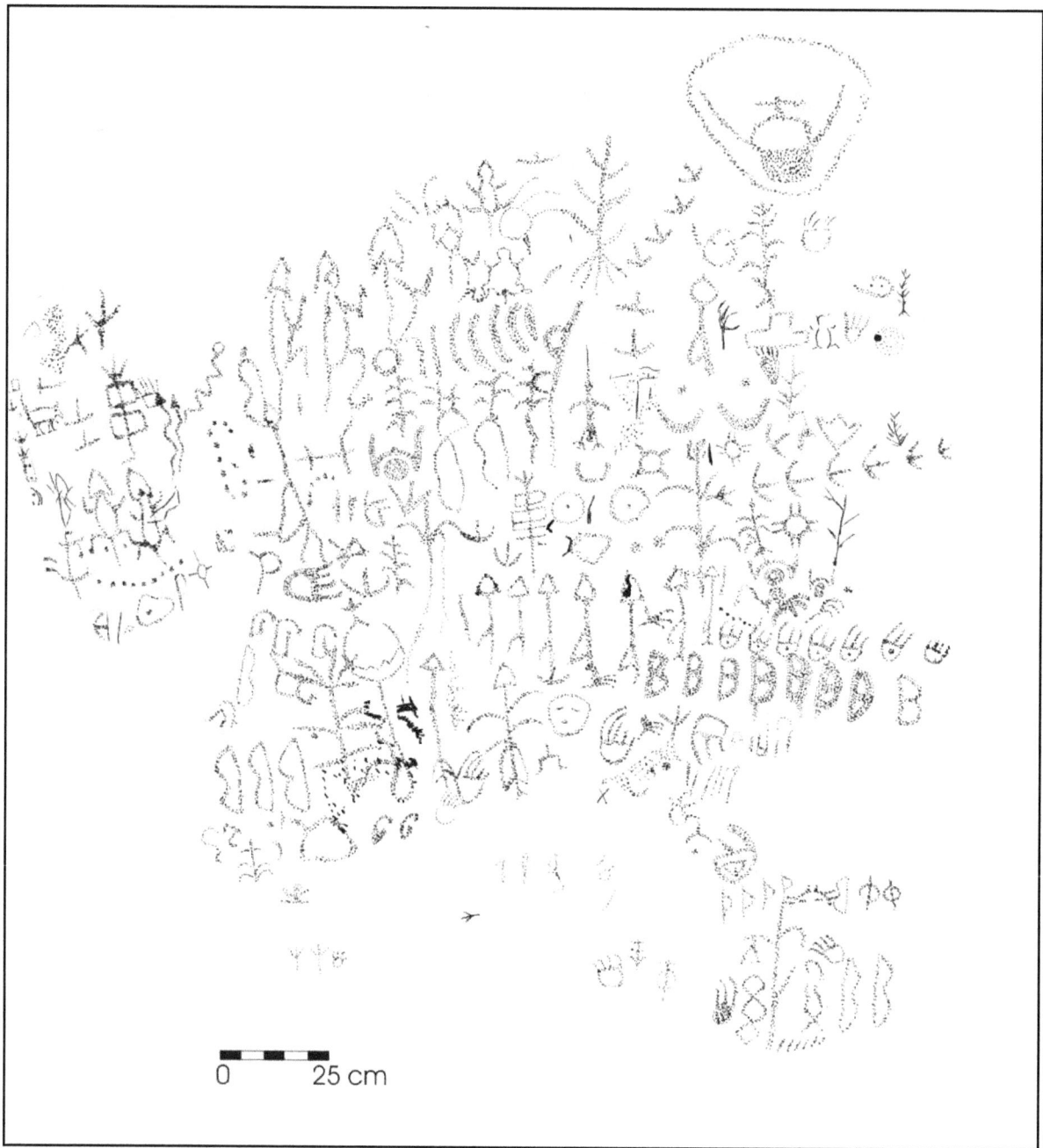

Figure I.68. Boulder 48 Southeast, left half (reconstructed using 1930 photographs); see DVD0974, 0976, 0978, 0984-1000, 1879, 1937-1941, 2059, 2064-2065, 2158, and 2512-2513.

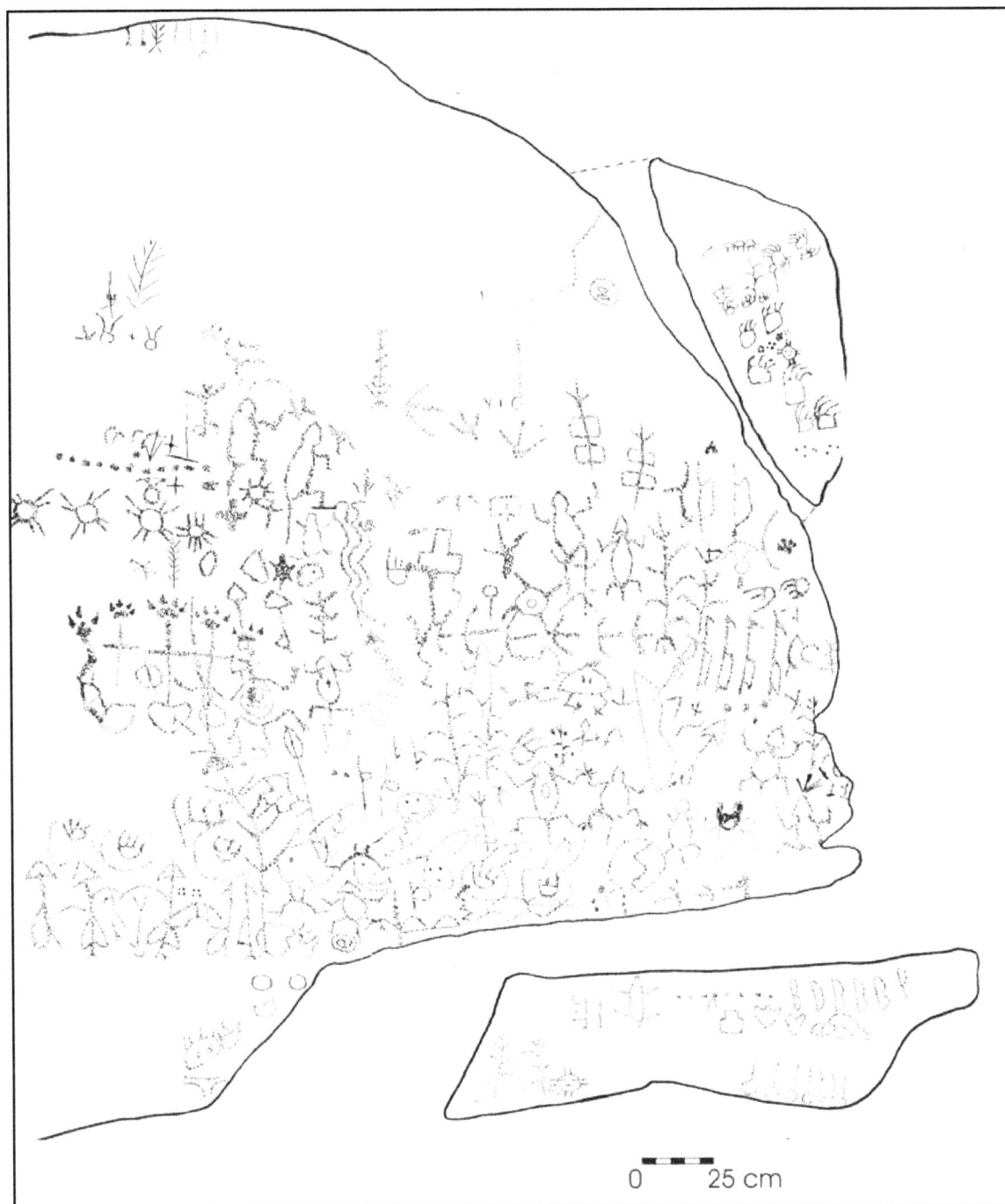

Figure I.69. Boulder 48 Southeast, right half (reconstructed using 1930 photographs); see DVD0977, 0979-0983, 1001-1019, 1936, 1996, 2056, 1060-1061, 2514, 2519, and 2521-2524.

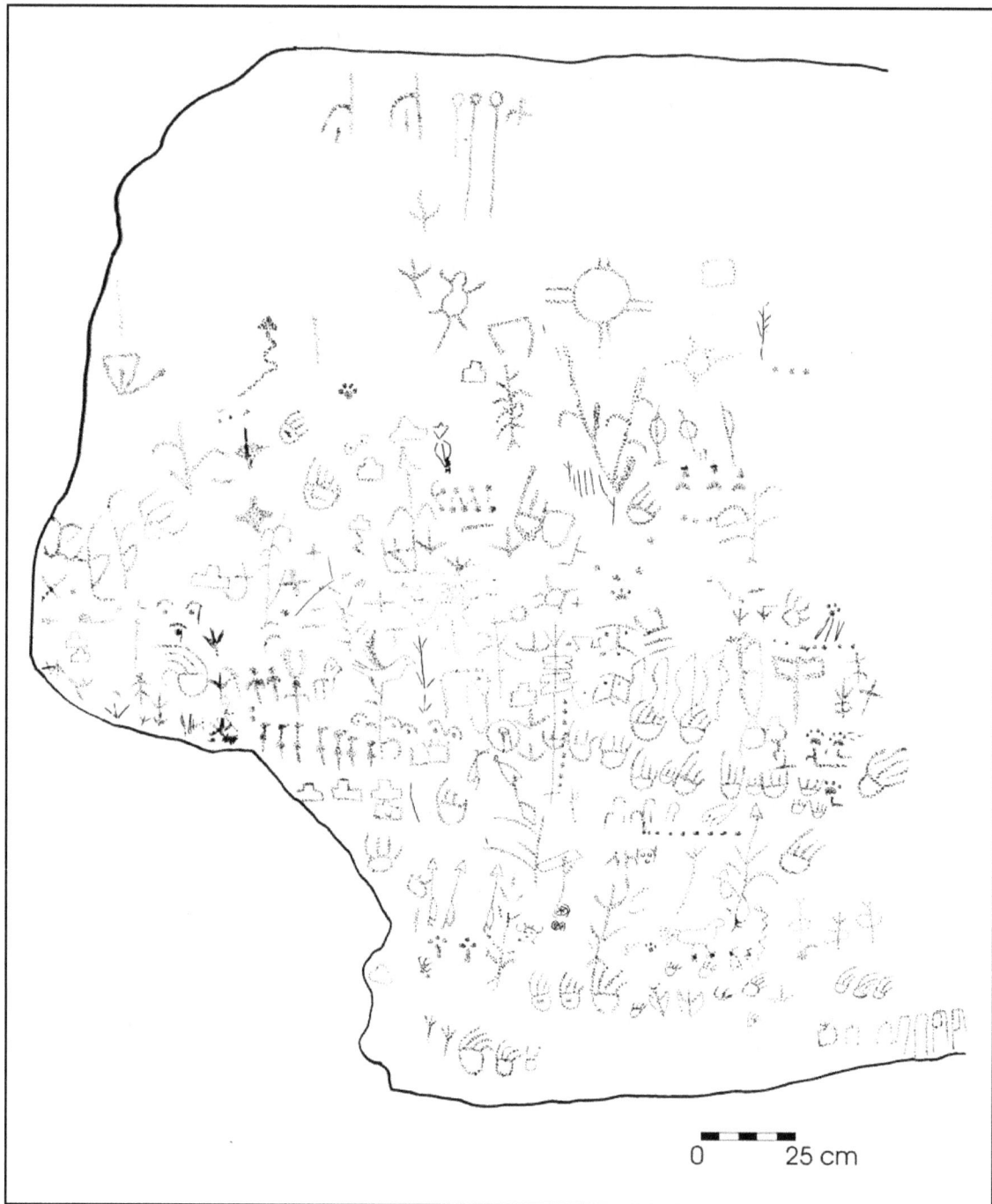

Figure I.70. Boulder 48 Southwest, left third (reconstructed using 1930 photographs); see DVD1020-1021, 1025-1026, 1028, 1030-1031, 1075-1080, 1091-1094, 1098, 1842, 1882, 1943-1946, 1952, 1955, 2067, 2069, 2074, 2402, 2415, 2525-2526, and 2561-2562.

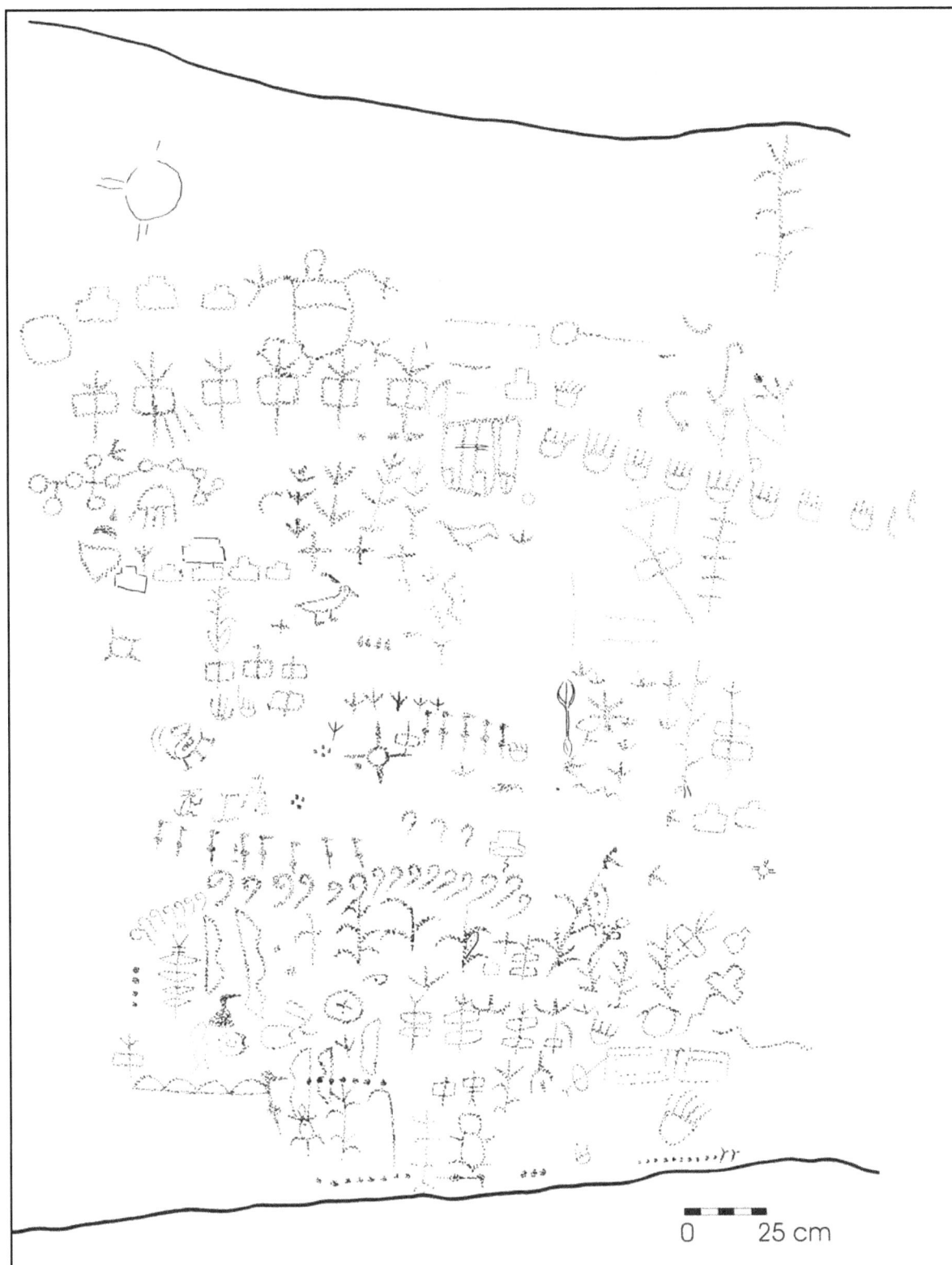

Figure I.71. Boulder 48 Southwest, middle third (reconstructed using 1930 photographs); see DVD1022, 1045-1053, 1072, 1081-1083, 1089-1090, 1947, 1950, 1953, 2068, 2070, 2073, and 2160.

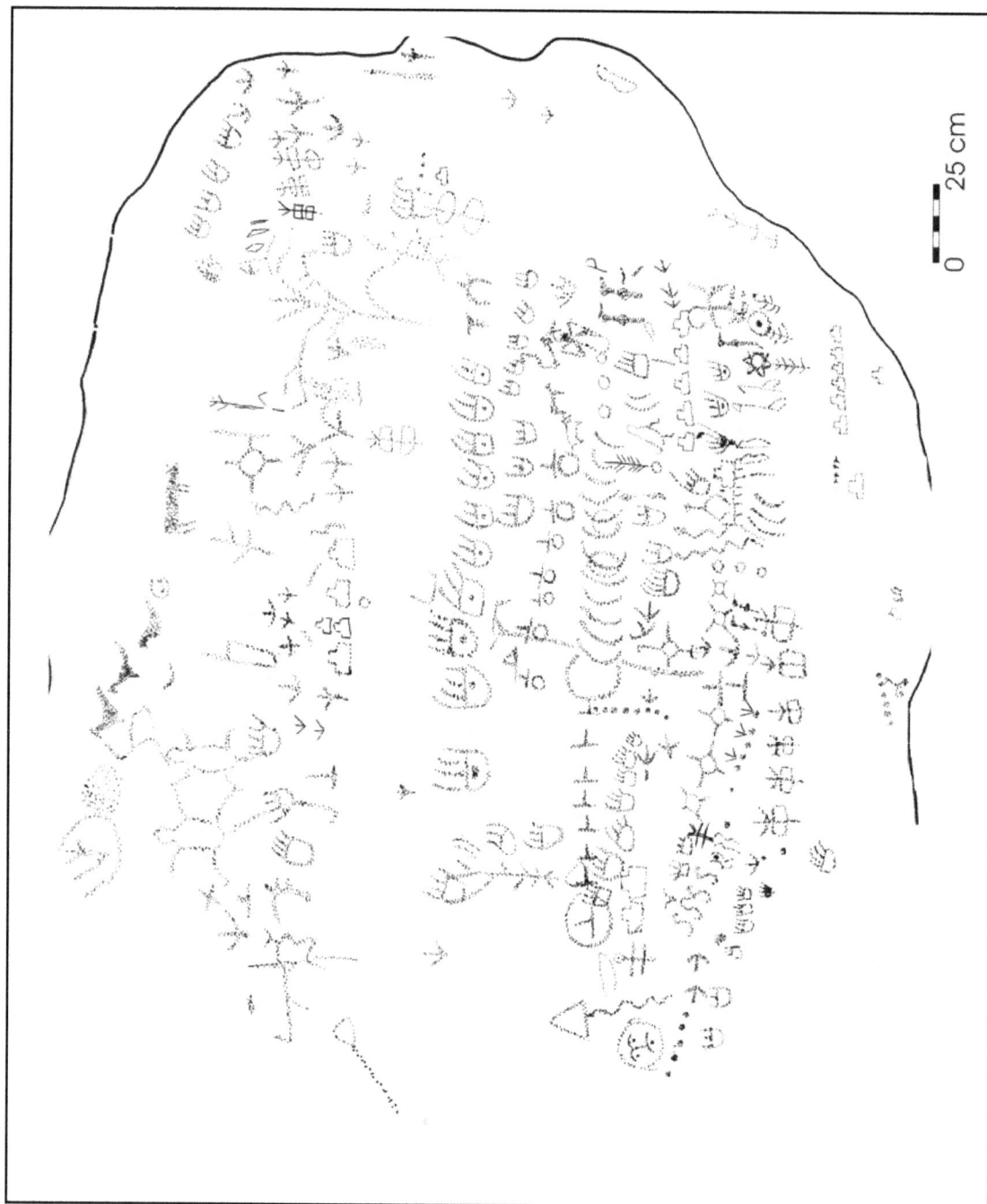

Figure I.72. Boulder 48 Southwest, right third (reconstructed using 1930 photographs); see DVD1023-1024, 1029, 1032-1035, 1054-1064, 1066-1071, 1073, 1084-1088, 1095-1097, 1099-1101, 1841, 1880-1881, 1948-1949, 1951, 1954, 2072, 2161, 2403, 2416, and 2527-2528.

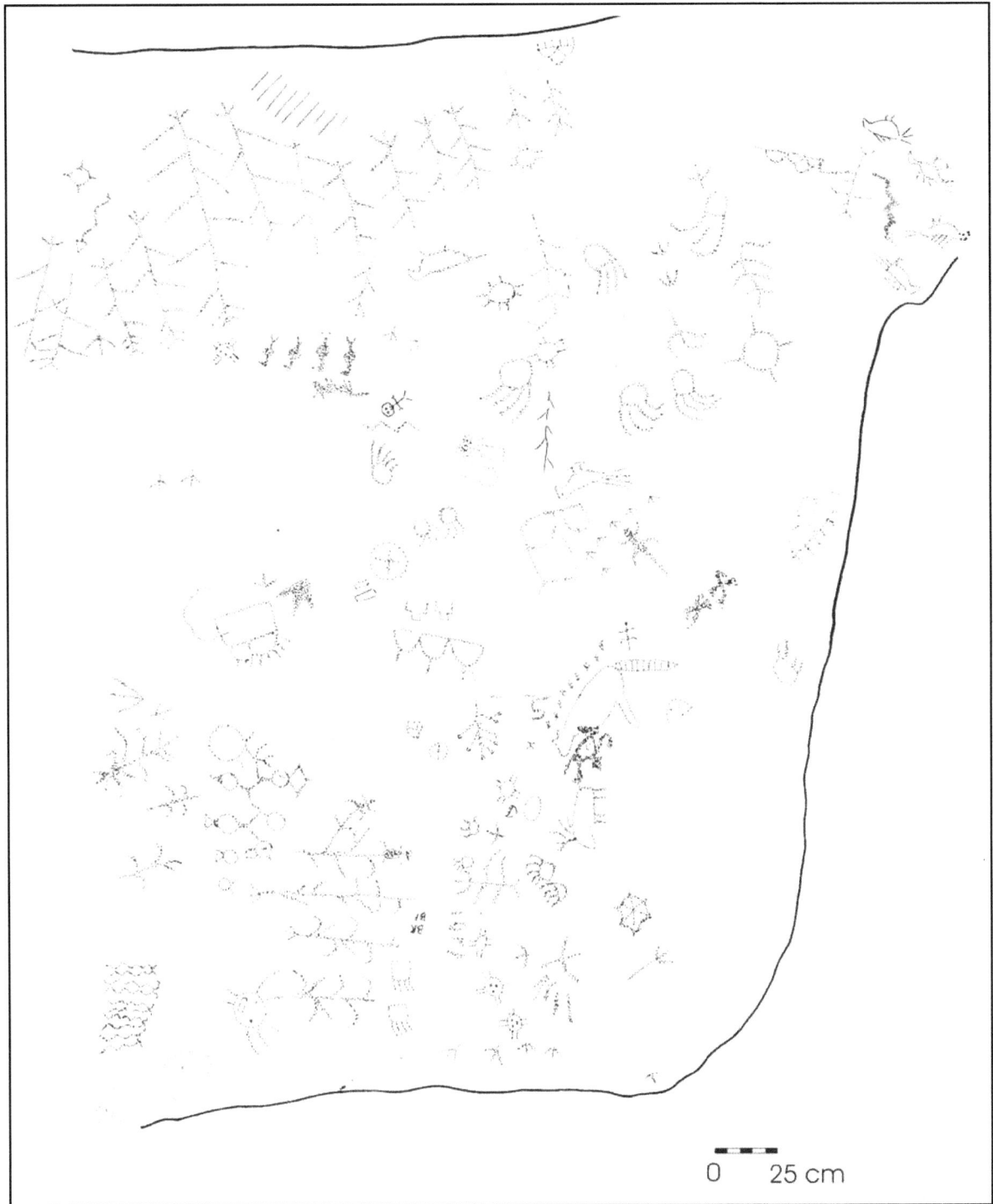

Figure I.73. Boulder 48 Top, north half; see DVD1102-1103, 1120, 1122-1128, and 1133.

Figure I.74. Boulder 48 Top, south half; see DVD 1104-1119, 1121, 1129, 1132, and 2077.

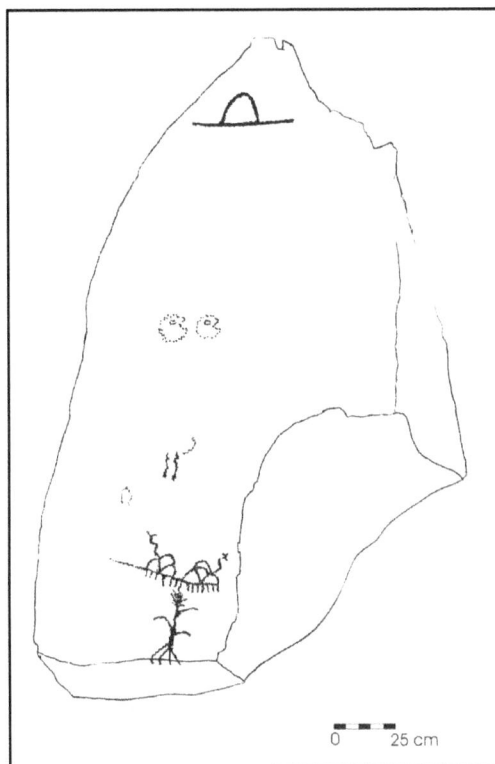

Figure I.75. Boulder 49 Northwest (reconstructed using 1984 photographs); see DVD1150-1155, 1956, 2000, and 2163.

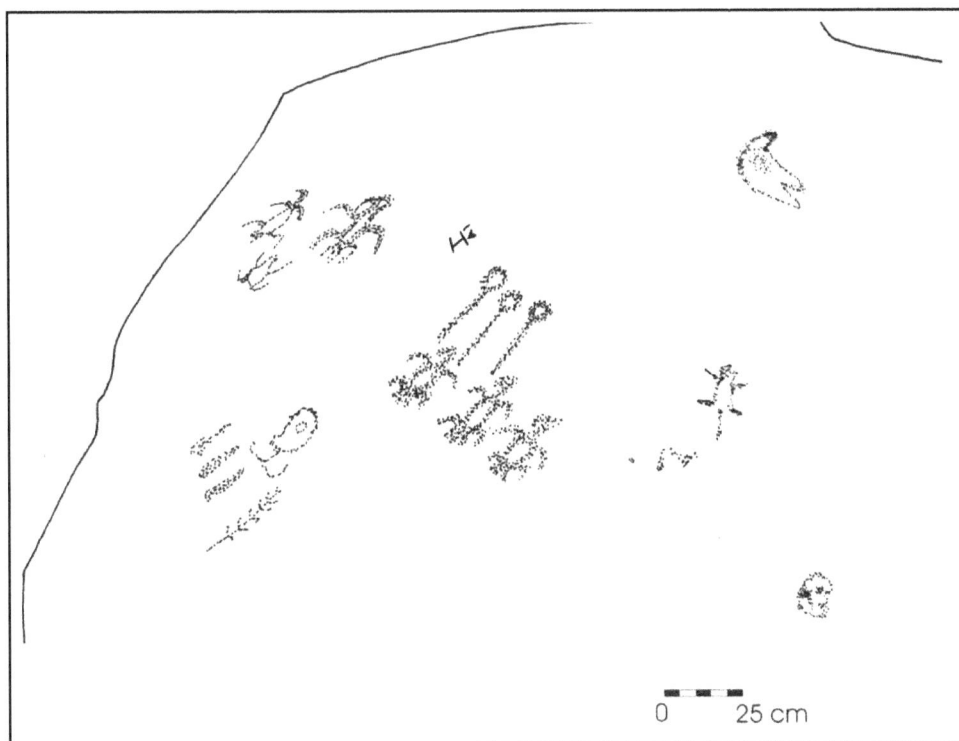

Figure I.76. Boulder 50 Top; see DVD1175-1190, 2167, and 2425.

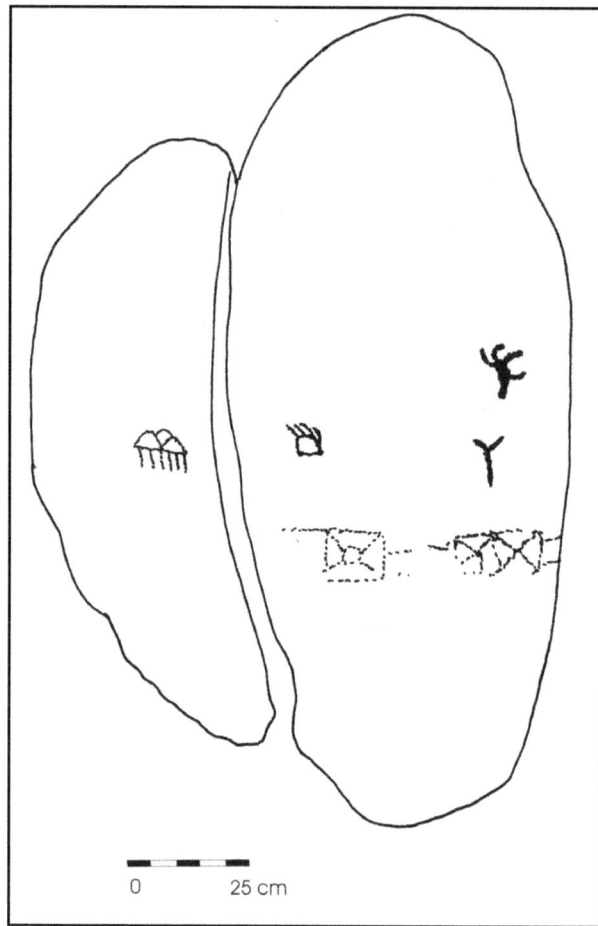

Figure I.77. Boulder 52 Top (reconstructed using 1978 photographs); see DVD1218-1223, 1885, 2001, 2119, 2168-2170, and 2426-2430.

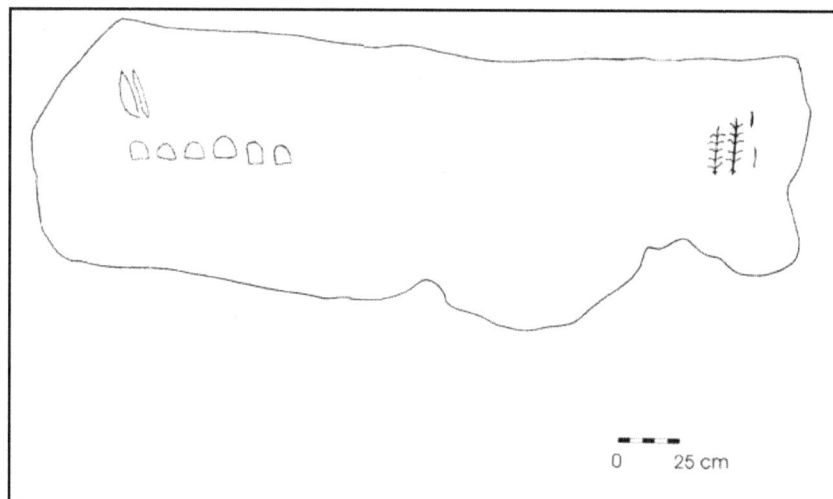

Figure I.78. Boulder 52 South; see DVD1212-1217.

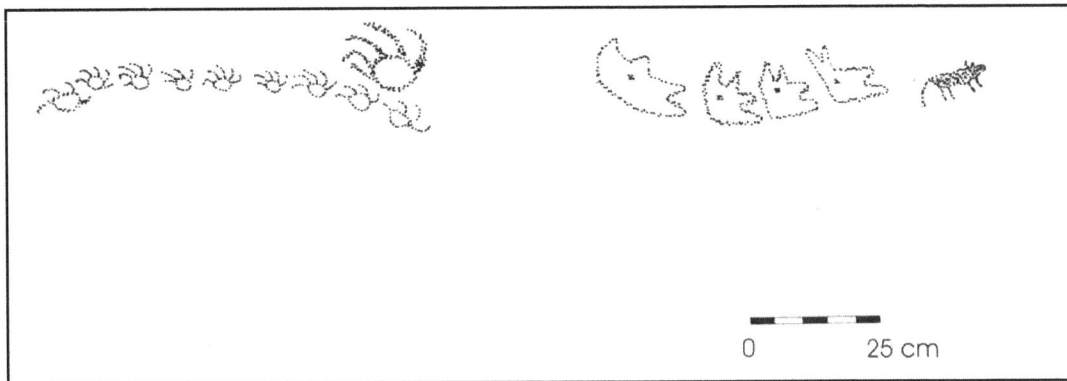

Figure I.79. Boulder 52 West (reconstructed using 1981 photographs); see DVD1224-1231, 1957-1958, 2093, 2171, and 2431.

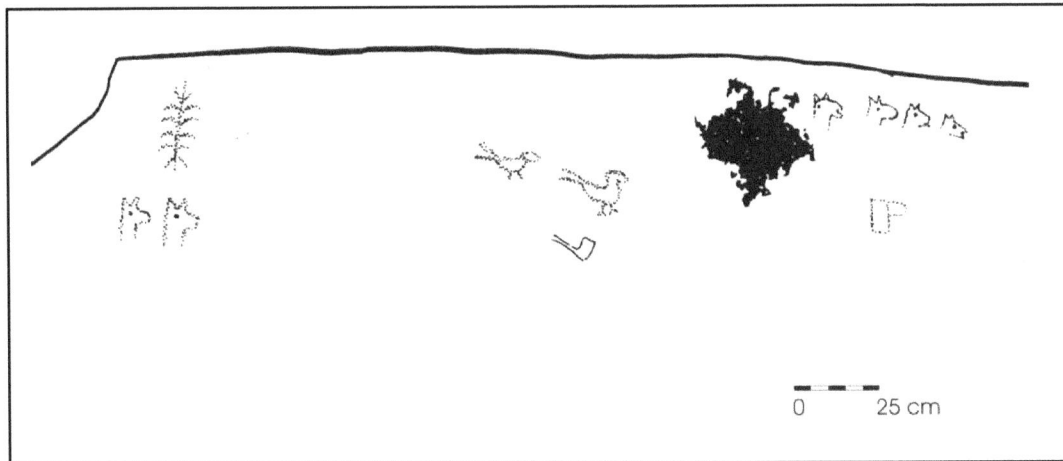

Figure I.80. Boulder 55 Northeast; see DVD1252-1260, 1888, and 2532-2533.

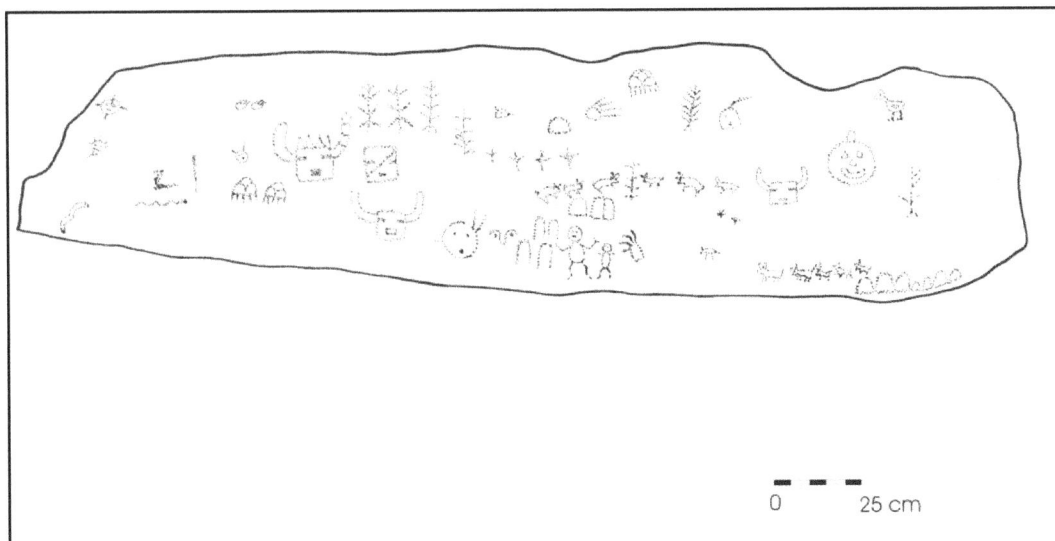

Figure I.81. Boulder 55 West (reconstructed using 1930 photographs); see DVD1284-1306, 1844-1848, 2002, 2173-2175, 2434-2438, and 2536-2538.

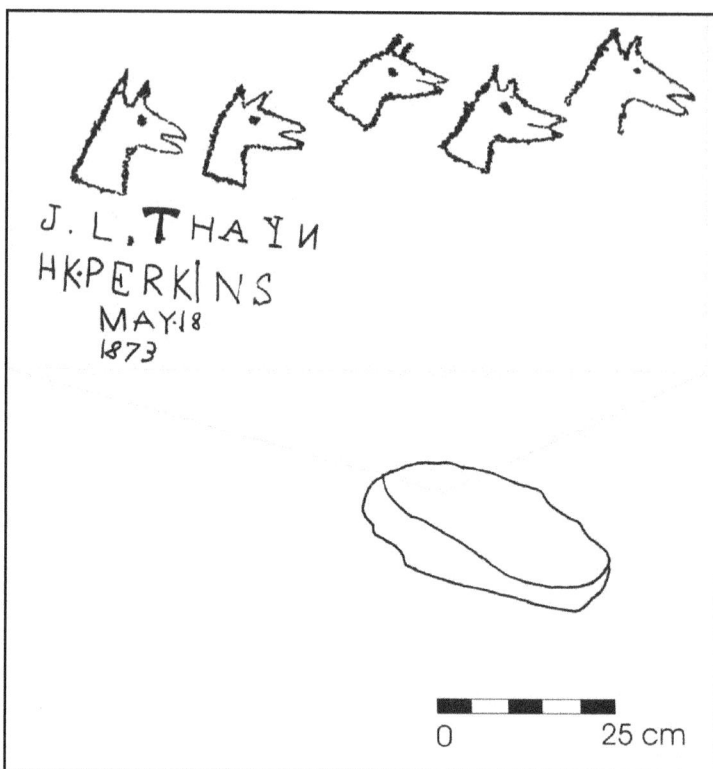

Figure I.82. Boulder 56 Top (reconstructed using 1978 photographs); see DVD1312-13147, 1889, and 2439.

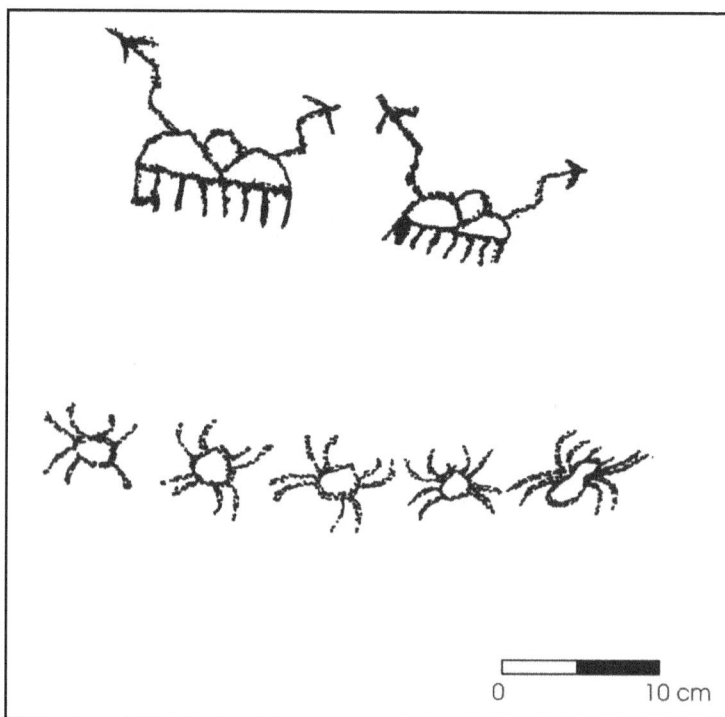

Figure I.83. Boulder 58 Top (reconstructed using 1981 photographs); see DVD1321-1330, 1960, 2440, and 2539.

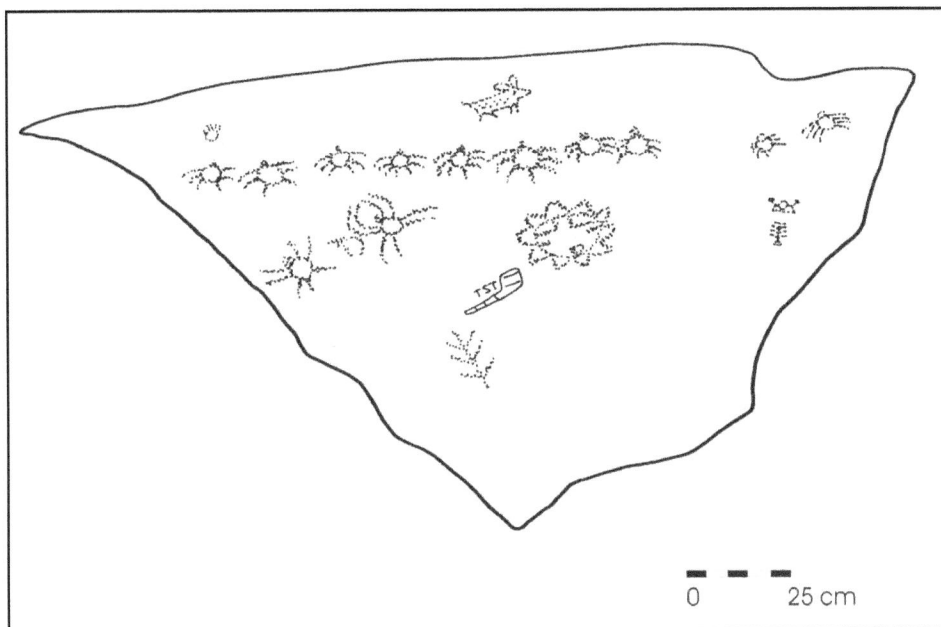

Figure I.84. Boulder 60 Top (reconstructed using 1978 photographs); see DVD1345-1355, 1891, 2003, 2079, 2176, 2442-2443, 2445, and 2541.

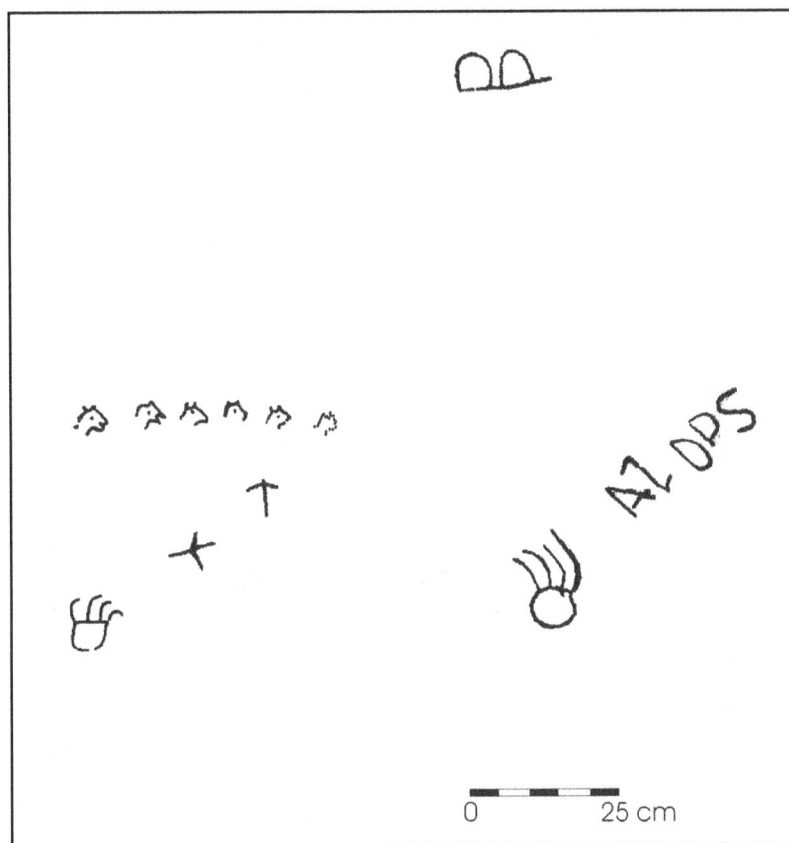

Figure I.85. Boulder 64 Top (reconstructed using 1978 photographs); see DVD1380-1386, 1892, and 2448.

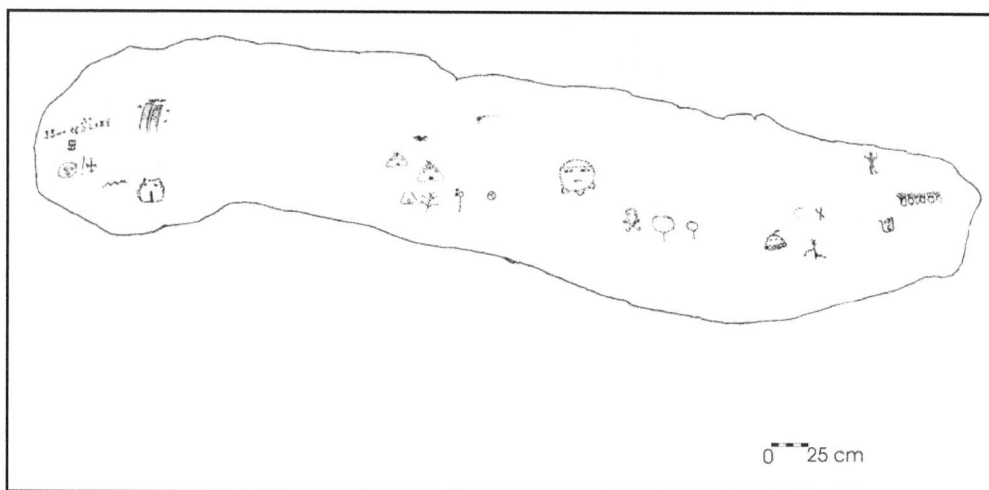

Figure I.86. Boulder 82 West (reconstructed using 1978 photographs); see DVD1473-1501, 1895, 1965-1968, 2083-2086, 2179-2180, and 2453-2459.

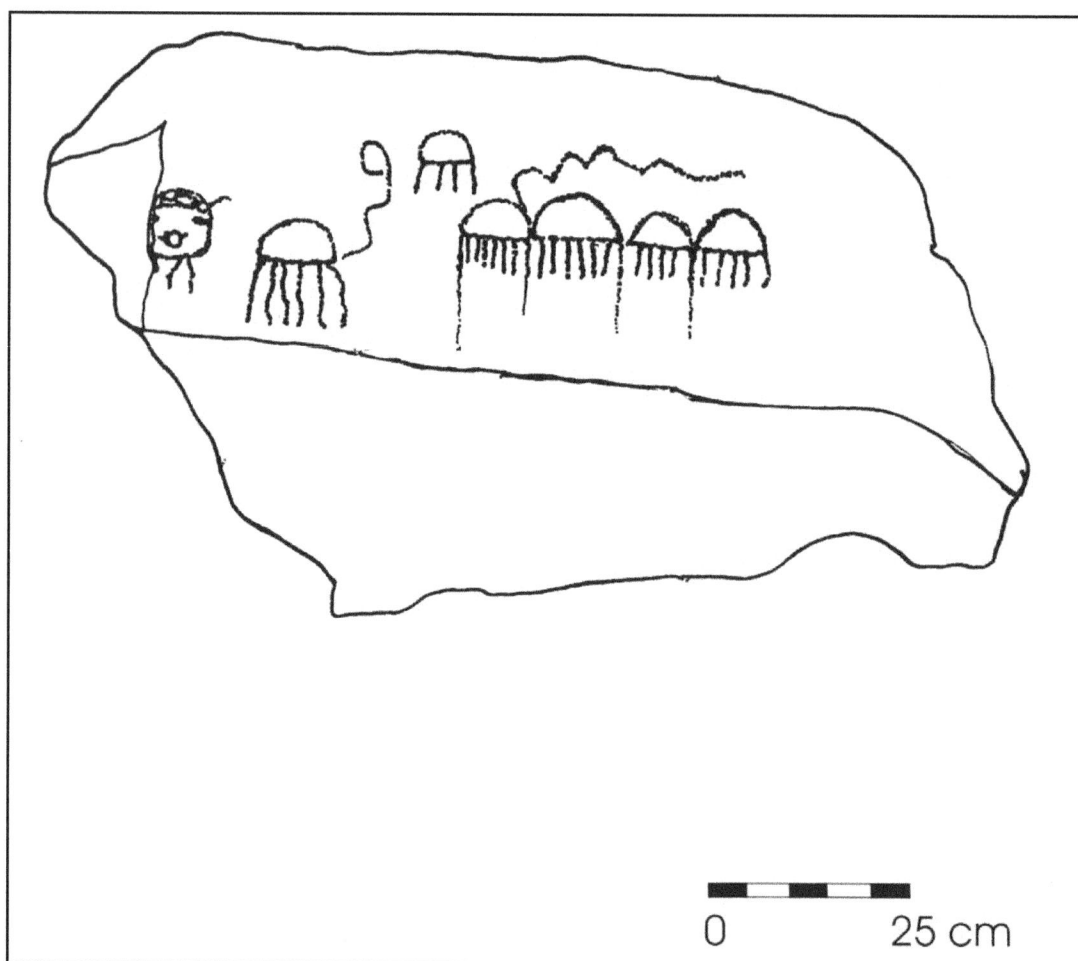

Figure I.87. Boulder 94 Southwest (reconstructed using 1981 photographs); see DVD1571-1578, 1971-1972, and 2462.

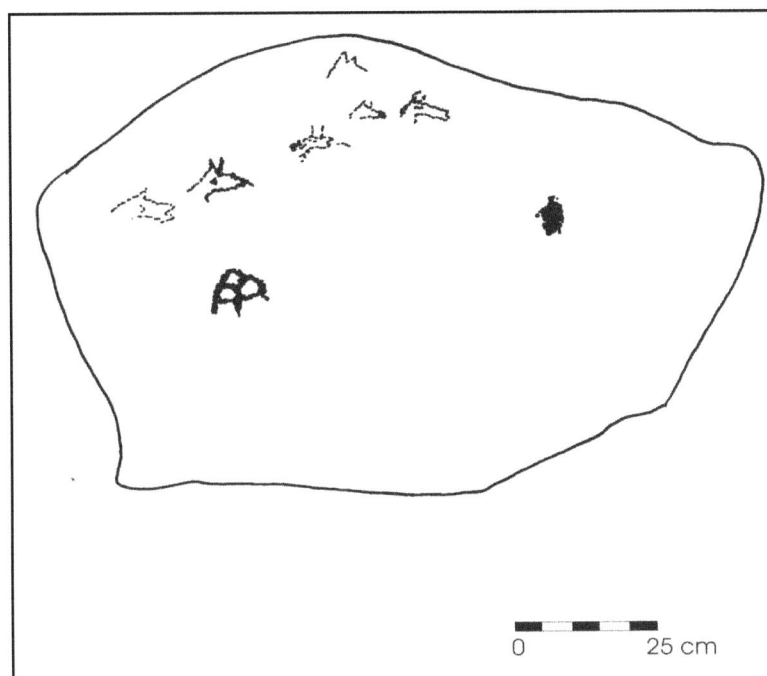

Figure I.88. Boulder 97 Southeast; see DVD1591-1596.

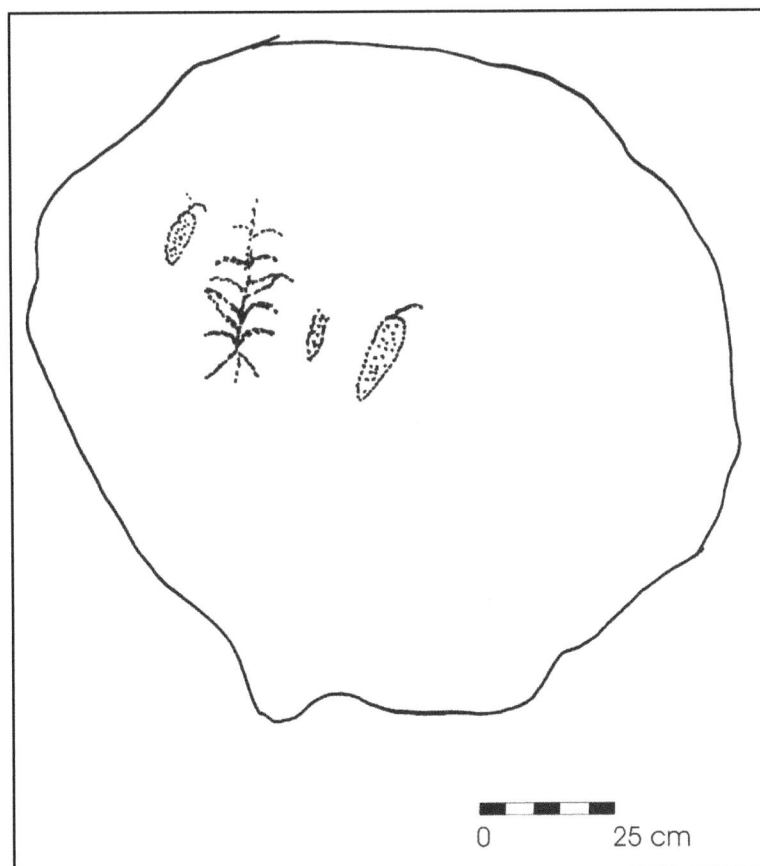

Figure I.89. Boulder 115 Northwest (reconstructed using 1978 photographs); see DVD1663-1670.

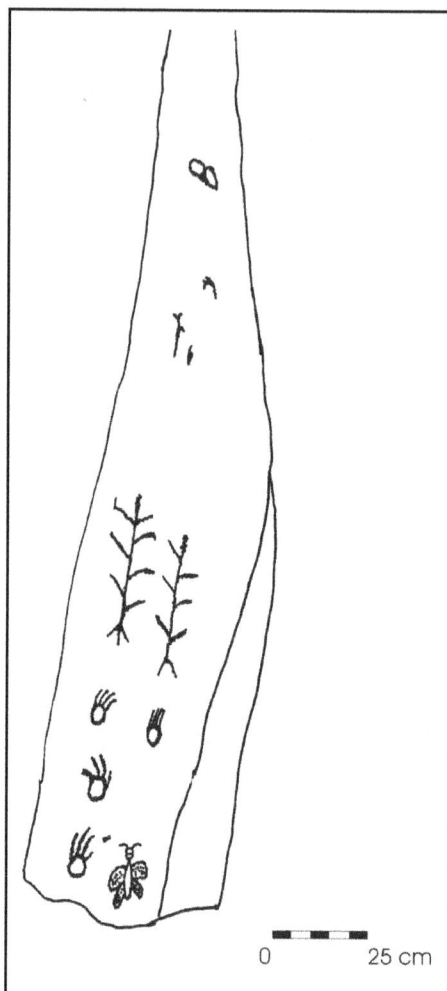

Figure I.90. Boulder 131 Top (reconstructed using 1984 photographs); see DVD1721-1724, 2007-2008, and 2466.

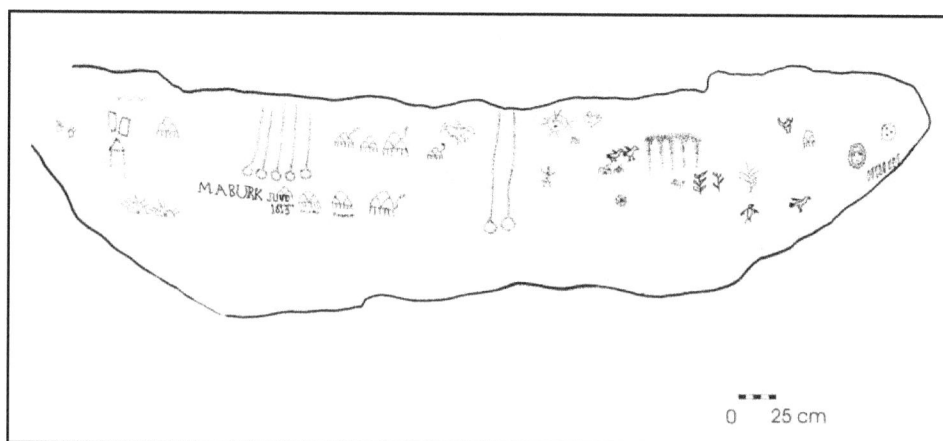

Figure I.91. Boulder 8 West (reconstructed using 1930 photographs). In text as Figure 3.7; see DVD0062-0122, 1805-1806, 1850-1851, 1898-1899, 1975-1976, 2009-2012, 2087, 2099-2103, 2121-2124, 2237-2252, and 2475-2476.

www.ingramcontent.com/pod-product-compliance
Lightning Source LLC
Chambersburg PA
CBHW080404270326

41927CB00015B/3345